**Other Books in the Turning Points Series:**

Turning
Points

IN WORLD HISTORY

# The French Revolution

David L. Bender, *Publisher*
Bruno Leone, *Executive Editor*
Bonnie Szumski, *Series Editor*
Don Nardo, *Book Editor*

Greenhaven Press, Inc., San Diego, California

Every effort has been made to trace the owners of copyrighted material. The articles in this volume may have been edited for content, length, and/or reading level. The titles have been changed to enhance the editorial purpose.

Library of Congress Cataloging-in-Publication Data

The French Revolution / Don Nardo, book editor.
     p.     cm. — (Turning points in world history)
    Includes bibliographical references and index.
    ISBN 1-56510-933-3 (pbk. : alk. paper). — ISBN 1-56510-934-1
(lib. bdg. : alk. paper)
    1. France—History—Revolution, 1789–1799. I. Nardo, Don,
1947–  . II. Series: Turning points in world history (Greenhaven
Press)
DC148.F715  1999
944.04—dc21                                   98-16604
                                                  CIP

Cover photo: Peter Newark's Historical Pictures

©1999 by Greenhaven Press, Inc.
P.O. Box 289009, San Diego, CA 92198-9009

Printed in the U.S.A.

# Contents

the Revolution its influence remains strong even today and the world will surely continue to feel its impact well into the future.

# Foreword

Certain past events stand out as pivotal, as having effects and outcomes that change the course of history. These events are often referred to as turning points. Historian Louis L. Snyder provides this useful definition:

> A turning point in history is an event, happening, or stage which thrusts the course of historical development into a different direction. By definition a turning point is a great event, but it is even more—a great event with the explosive impact of altering the trend of man's life on the planet.

History's turning points have taken many forms. Some were single, brief, and shattering events with immediate and obvious impact. The invasion of Britain by William the Conqueror in 1066, for example, swiftly transformed that land's political and social institutions and paved the way for the rise of the modern English nation. By contrast, other single events were deemed of minor significance when they occurred, only later recognized as turning points. The assassination of a little-known European nobleman, Archduke Franz Ferdinand, on June 28, 1914, in the Bosnian town of Sarajevo was such an event; only after it touched off a chain reaction of political-military crises that escalated into the global conflict known as World War I did the murder's true significance become evident.

Other crucial turning points occurred not in terms of a few hours, days, months, or even years, but instead as evolutionary developments spanning decades or even centuries. One of the most pivotal turning points in human history, for instance—the development of agriculture, which replaced nomadic hunter-gatherer societies with more permanent settlements—occurred over the course of many generations. Still other great turning points were neither events nor developments, but rather revolutionary new inventions and innovations that significantly altered social customs and ideas, military tactics, home life, the spread of knowledge, and the human condition in general. The developments of writing, gunpowder, the printing press, antibiotics, the electric light, atomic energy, television, and the computer, the last two of which have recently ushered in the world-altering information age, represent only some of these innovative turning points.

Each anthology in the Greenhaven Turning Points in World History series presents a group of essays chosen for their accessibility. The anthology's structure also enhances this accessibility. First, an introductory essay provides a general overview of the principal events and figures involved, placing the topic in its historical context. The essays that follow explore various aspects in more detail, some targeting political trends and consequences, others social, literary, cultural, and/or technological ramifications, and still others pivotal leaders and other influential figures. To aid the reader in choosing the material of immediate interest or need, each essay is introduced by a concise summary of the contributing writer's main themes and insights.

In addition, each volume contains extensive research tools, including a collection of excerpts from primary source documents pertaining to the historical events and figures under discussion. In the anthology on the French Revolution, for example, readers can examine the works of Rousseau, Voltaire, and other writers and thinkers whose championing of human rights helped fuel the French people's growing desire for liberty; the French *Declaration of the Rights of Man and Citizen*, presented to King Louis XVI by the French National Assembly on October 2, 1789; and eyewitness accounts of the attack on the royal palace and the horrors of the Reign of Terror. To guide students interested in pursuing further research on the subject, each volume features an extensive bibliography, which for easy access has been divided into separate sections by topic. Finally, a comprehensive index allows readers to scan and locate content efficiently. Each of the anthologies in the Greenhaven Turning Points in World History series provides students with a complete, detailed, and enlightening examination of a crucial historical watershed.

# Introduction: In the Shadow of the Revolution

The French Revolution has been variously called a great turning point, a watershed, and a point of departure at which the traditional social and political institutions of premodern Europe began to give way to powerful new forces and ideas. The American Revolution, which had given birth to the United States in the 1770s, had been driven by liberal notions of social equality and political liberty, the desire for justice and democratic institutions, and a strong spirit of national identity. Beginning in 1789, these same forces and ideas swept away France's old political-social order, the so-called ancien régime; and over the course of the following decade, revolutionary turmoil transformed all sectors of French society and involved or affected every major state in Europe. In fact, writes distinguished historian William Doyle,

> the shadow of the Revolution fell across the whole of the nineteenth century and beyond. Until 1917 [when the Russian Revolution began] few would have disputed that it was the greatest revolution in the history of the world; and even after that its claims to primacy remain strong. It was the first modern revolution, the archetypical one. After it, nothing in the European world remained the same, and we are all heirs to its influence.[1]

## The Social Pyramid

The immediate chain of events leading to the French Revolution began in the late 1750s and early 1760s when France squared off against Britain in the Seven Years' War (called the French and Indian War in America). France lost the war and along with it valuable North American lands and markets. Subsequent royal financial mismanagement and self-indulgence worsened the situation. King Louis XV, who died in 1774, wasted large sums on costly wars and personal luxuries while failing to effect the tax reforms and other measures needed to replenish the treasury and maintain a sound budget. His most lasting achievement was to alienate a majority of the French people and to make them resent and distrust the monarchy.

Such bitterness toward Louis and his government only heightened the social and political unrest that had been growing for some time in France. The social structure of the ancien régime was rigid, in many ways class oriented and unjust, and increasingly outmoded, and members of all social classes, for a variety of reasons, had become uncomfortable and unhappy with the status quo. A noted historian of the Revolution, George Rudé, explains:

> We may picture French eighteenth-century society as a kind of pyramid, whose apex was filled by the Court and aristocracy, its center by the "middling" classes, or bourgeoisie [mostly shopkeepers and businessmen], and its base by the "lower orders" of [rural] peasants and urban tradesmen and craftsmen.

This structure in itself was nothing new or unusual and constituted the basic model of all European societies of the time. What, then, made French society different from the others, and ominously so, considering that France became Europe's seedbed for violent revolution and social change? Rudé continues:

> The French social pyramid was riddled with contradictions both within and between its constituent parts. For it had a monarchy that, although absolute in theory, carried within it the seeds of its own decay; an aristocracy that, though privileged and mostly wealthy, was deeply resentful of its long exclusion from office; a bourgeoisie that, though enjoying increasing prosperity, was denied the social status and share in government commensurate with its wealth; and peasants who (in part at least) were becoming more literate and independent, yet were still regarded as a general beast of burden, despised and over-taxed. Moreover, these conflicts and the tensions they engendered were becoming sharper as the century went on.[2]

These social conflicts and tensions finally reached the breaking point during the reign of Louis XV's successor, Louis XVI. The new king, formally crowned at Rheims cathedral on June 11, 1775, was a well-meaning but indecisive and ultimately ineffectual ruler who was unable to halt the erosion of public confidence in the traditional government. Under his rule, the national treasury continued to shrink until, by 1787, it was virtually empty and the government was deeply in debt; indeed, on the eve of the Revolution, nearly half of the yearly royal budget had to be allocated solely to paying the interest on that debt.

## The Estates General

For years, one financial minister after another had advised Louis that putting the economy back on its feet would require tapping into the wealth of the nobility and church, primarily through a tax on land. At the time, both the aristocracy and clergy were exempt from land taxes, and these two influential landholding classes repeatedly balked at any change in that status. The only legal way that Louis and his government could force payment was by convening a meeting of the Estates General. This body was the French version of medieval Europe's great councils, in which leading citizens had met periodically with rulers to consider important matters of state (in England, such councils had evolved into the representative legislature known as Parliament). As medieval France had grown into an absolute monarchy in the 1400s and 1500s, the Estates General had decreased in influence and importance. Its last meeting had taken place in 1614, more than a century and a half before Louis ascended the throne.

Now in dire need of money, Louis called a new meeting of the Estates General on May 5, 1789, in Versailles, near Paris. This move demonstrated the king's desperation and weakened authority; it also raised many people's hopes that the government might finally be forced to consider the longstanding grievances of various social groups. According to scholar R.K. Gooch:

> The summoning of the Estates General was a recognition of the fact that reform was imperative. It was also a recognition of the fact that the king could not, without the collaboration of the nation, effect real reform. . . . The king's acceptance, however reluctant, of the direction and force of public opinion aroused high hopes in the country.[3]

Despite the fact that he was dealing from a position of weakness, Louis maintained a superior, arrogant attitude. Apparently, he expected the assembled delegates to bow to his wishes automatically and vote to raise the funds he needed.

Events did not transpire as the king had planned, however. First, the various delegates arrived at the conference carrying *cahiers de doléances*, lists of grievances they intended to present to Louis and force him to address. Such lists had been drawn up by delegates representing each of the three estates, or classes, of society. The clergy constituted the first estate, the nobles the second estate, and the common people (including the bourgeoisie, despite the fact that some were very well-to-do) the third estate. Typical of the demands of the *cahiers* were calls for regular meetings of the Estates General, less oppressive taxes, and a free press. The group calling itself the Third Estate of the City of Paris, for instance, demanded that "liberty of the press must be granted, on condition that authors sign their manuscripts, that the printer's name shall appear, and that both shall be responsible for the consequences of publication."[4]

## Creation of the National Assembly

Before such grievances and demands could be addressed, however, the members had to agree on a workable procedure for debate and voting. The third estate, whose members were the most numerous and clamorous for social reform, immediately made it plain that they were a force to be reckoned with. "What is the third estate?" asked the popular pamphleteer Abbé Sieyès shortly before the meeting. "Everything," he answered. "What has it been hitherto [before] in the political order? Nothing. What does it demand? To be something."[5]

Inspired by these defiant and ambitious words, the leaders of the third estate started a loud argument over the voting procedure. According to tradition, each estate had a single, collective voice; but the third estate objected to this arrangement, arguing quite correctly that the privileged clergy and nobles would, as they had so often in the past, always vote together, two to one, against them. The commoners demanded that the rules be changed to give each and every delegate a vote. Since the clergy had 308 delegates, the nobles 285, and the commoners 621, the third estate would then have a majority voice.

When the first and second estates refused to change the voting rules, the members of the third angrily walked out of the meeting. Soon afterward, on June 17, 1789, they held their own meeting and, claiming that they represented the wishes of most French citizens, boldly declared themselves the National Assembly of France. Convening three days later at a local tennis court, they took the famous "Tennis Court Oath," which read in part:

> Be it resolved that all members of this Assembly immediately take solemn oath never to separate, and to reassemble whenever circumstances require, until the constitution of the kingdom is established and fixed upon firm foundations; and that the said oath being taken, all members in general, and each in particular, shall confirm by their signatures, this irrevocable resolution.[6]

The Revolution had begun.

## The Bastille and the Great Fear

It is important to emphasize that at the time the members of the new National Assembly did not intend to make France a democracy; nor did they conceive of eliminating the monarchy. They simply hoped to draft a written constitution that would guarantee all French citizens, regardless of social class, basic civil rights, and then oblige the king to agree to and sign the document. That would make France a constitutional monarchy, in which the king's authority rested on the will of the people and their legislative representatives. At first, the king ordered that the Assembly desist from its impudent actions; however, a number of reform-minded clergymen and nobles soon joined the commoners and Louis saw no other choice than to give in. On June 27, 1789, he formally requested all three estates to meet and to vote by person rather than by group. Had nothing else happened to upset this scenario, the grievances of all groups might have been considered and resolved and violent revolution might have been avoided.

Louis soon bungled the situation, however. Influenced by members of the royal family and a few disgruntled conservative aristocrats, all of whom feared losing their power and wealth, in early summer the king ordered troops to begin massing in the outskirts of Versailles and Paris. This move caused extreme anxiety in the streets of the capital. Worried that the troops might disband the Assembly or perhaps attack the city, many people in Paris and neighboring towns began collecting arms.

On July 14, the search for weapons led a large crowd to march to the Bastille, the fortress-prison in which the government had once kept its political prisoners, an edifice that had come to be seen as a hated symbol of the monarchy's past abuses. Unfortunately, the governor of the fortress, out of fear and ineptitude, ordered his guards to fire on the crowd; ninety-eight people were killed and many others wounded. Hundreds of the angry survivors then captured the fortress and executed the governor and several of his men. Ever since, July 14, called Bastille Day, has been celebrated as France's independence day.

Following the Bastille's fall, similar uprisings and demonstrations against the government broke out in other parts of the country. Rumors spread that the king was ordering his troops into rural areas to suppress dissent by the peasants, the most numerous members of the third estate. Swept along by what became known as the "Great Fear," many peasants burned rich mansions and destroyed records and documents listing their ancient feudal obligations to provide aristocratic landlords with labor and monetary payments. Moved by these demonstrations, in a dramatic gesture on the night of

August 4 the aristocrats in the Assembly renounced their feudal rights. From that moment on, all French citizens were theoretically equal under the law.

This preliminary establishment of equality paved the way for the Assembly to draft its long-awaited constitution. On August 27, it issued what was intended as the first section of that document, the Declaration of the Rights of Man and Citizen. "The representatives of the French people," the document began,

> constituted as a National Assembly, and considering that ignorance, neglect, or contempt of the rights of man are the sole causes of public misfortunes and governmental corruption, have resolved to set forth in a solemn declaration the natural, inalienable, and sacred rights of man.[7]

The declaration went on to list basic civil rights, each stirring phrase echoing the sentiments of Englishman John Locke, Swiss-Frenchman Jean-Jacques Rousseau, and other political-social philosophers who had also inspired the American founding fathers. Like the American Bill of Rights, the French version established specific civil liberties, including the right to be presumed innocent until proven guilty, equality of all citizens under the law, and freedom of religion.

## The New Constitution

Hoping for the king's approval, the leaders of the Assembly presented the declaration to Louis on October 2, 1789. They were disappointed, however, when he stalled judgment on its merits until some later, unspecified time. The longer he hesitated, the more suspicions grew that he might again call out troops to stop the revolutionary process; at the same time, bread shortages, a common occurrence of late, continued, intensifying public unrest. On October 5, a large crowd of Parisian women marched to Louis's palace at Versailles to demand bread and ended up occupying the grounds all night. Under this pressure, the king gave in and agreed to accept the Assembly's decrees. But the growing crowd did not trust his word and forced him and his family to move to the old palace, the Tuileries, in Paris, where his subjects could keep an eye on him. Joseph Weber, foster brother of the queen, Marie-Antoinette, witnessed the march back to Paris and later recalled "the horror of a cold, somber, rainy day, the infamous militia splattering through the mud, the harpies, monsters with human faces [i.e., the commoners in the crowd], the captive monarch and his family . . . dragged along by guards."[8]

The royal family remained under close watch for more than a year while the Assembly finished drafting the new constitution. According to this document, France was to be a constitutional monarchy. The king would be the head of state but would have to answer to a national legislature, in which all real legal and political authority would reside. Thus, Louis would be unable to declare war, make peace, or perform any other important acts without the approval of the legislature. The Assembly also abolished the ancient French provinces and in their place set up eighty-three local areas of roughly equal size called departments, each subdivided into smaller units designated districts and communes. In addition, the metric system was introduced to provide the country with uniform weights and measures and the educational system was overhauled to serve the needs of the new, classless society.

The Assembly took an even more controversial step. To help pay off the national debt incurred by Louis and his predecessors, the new government began confiscating lands owned by the Roman Catholic Church, a move that greatly angered the clergy. In March 1791, the pope condemned the seizures as an attack on the clergy, and many French people, feeling forced to choose between patriotism and religious conviction, suffered a crisis of conscience that undermined the unity that the government needed to make its sweeping reconstruction of the nation work.

The pope and his most devout followers were not the only enemies the revolutionary leaders made. Many conservative aristocrats, dismayed by the loss of their privileged positions, fled France and settled in neighboring countries, where they tried to stir up counterrevolution that would restore France to its former state. Among these so-called émigrés was the king's younger brother, the count of Artois. The count persuaded Louis and his family to attempt escape; on the night of June 20, 1791, they disguised themselves as servants and headed for northeastern France, there to seek the protection of a force of French and foreign troops. But the revolutionary authorities caught the royal family in the act and returned them to Paris. There, angry crowds denounced Louis as a traitor and called for his removal.

## The Jacobins and the Republic

Its task of restructuring the government and administration completed, in September 1791 the Assembly disbanded itself to make way for the new Legislative Assembly, created in the constitution, which first met on October 1. It immediately became clear that the new Assembly was even more radical in its beliefs and goals than the old one. This was due to the influence of a left-wing political club, or clique, known as the Jacobins, who were determined to root out and crush all counterrevolutionary forces and to replace the constitutional monarchy with a more democratic republic.[9] As historian Arthur May explains, the Jacobins were divided into two groups who over time came increasingly to oppose each other:

> Much the larger group was called the Girondins [or Girondists], spokesmen of the provinces, noble idealists and elegant orators, but short on discipline and on leaders capable of leading. The Girondins understood ideas better than they understood human nature. Competing with them were the deputies of the "Mountain" [or Montagnards], backed by extremist political clubs and radical newspapers of Paris and lesser cities. . . . These men were the . . . champions of the wretched city folk. At their head were two stalwart Jacobins, Georges-Jacques Danton and Maximilien Robespierre, bourgeois lawyers both, spokesmen of the urban masses by choice, domineering, skillful pilots of men.[10]

At first, the Girondins assumed leadership of the government and one of their first acts was to demand that all émigrés return to France at once or lose their property. When it became clear that this demand would not be met, on April 20, 1792, the leaders boldly declared war on Austria, Marie-Antoinette's homeland and a hotbed of counterrevolutionary activities. Soon, France found itself facing Austria's ally, Prussia, too. The war radicalized the revolution. When the leader of the Prussian forces threatened to level Paris if the king came to harm, angry crowds broke into the Tuileries, forcing the royal family to take refuge in the Legislative Assembly itself; and subsequently, another mob massacred over twelve hundred prisoners in the city jails, mistaking them for counterrevolutionaries. An extreme left-wing journalist named Jean Paul Marat, whose newspaper, *The Friend of the People*, had became immensely popular with the urban poor in the preceding two years, played a crucial role in inciting these killings.

Eventually, the extreme Jacobins of the Mountain joined forces with a group of disgruntled Parisian shopkeepers, artisans, and factory workers known as the *sans-culottes*.[11] On September 21, 1792, the day after a French army halted the Prussian advance into western France, they convened what they named the Convention and declared the nation a republic. The monarchy was now defunct and the presence of its former royalty an embarrassment to the new radical leaders. In December, they put Louis on trial; despite Girondin efforts to save him, he was condemned to death and beheaded on January 21, 1793.

## The Reign of Terror

Less than a month later, blindly hoping to export the Revolution to other countries and transform Europe, the Convention declared war on Britain, Holland, and Spain; before long France stood alone against every major European power. Fearing uprisings in their own societies, these powers instituted highly repressive domestic policies.[12] The Mountain, which now controlled France, faced the daunting task of fighting the huge foreign coalition while simultaneously trying to govern the nation and maintain its dominance over rival political factions.

To deal with these challenges, Mountain leaders created a series of "committees," the most important of which, the

Committee of Public Safety, soon exercised almost complete dictatorial power. The most prominent members of this group were Danton, Robespierre, and Lazare Carnot, who took charge of the military. Although Marat, who still enjoyed a wide public following, did not belong to any specific group or committee, he sympathized with and backed the Mountain. When he was stabbed to death on July 13, 1793, by a young woman backing the Girondins, the Committee's leaders exploited the crime to gain support for themselves and discredit their Girondin opponents.

Justifying its actions as absolutely necessary in the face of an extreme national emergency, the Committee of Public Safety employed blatantly undemocratic, often brutal means to get its way; thus ensued the infamous Reign of Terror (or simply "the Terror"), which lasted from autumn 1793 to midsummer 1794. The main instrument of the Terror was a series of revolutionary tribunals in which "enemies" of the republic were arrested and in many cases executed. In the name of national security, the Convention provided a means for identifying enemies in the form of the Law of Suspects (passed in September 1793), which read in part:

> The following are deemed suspected persons: those who, by their conduct, associations, talk, or writings have shown themselves partisans of tyranny or federalism and enemies of liberty . . . those to whom certificates of patriotism have been refused . . . those former nobles, husbands, wives, fathers, mothers, sons or daughters . . . and agents of the émigrés, who have not steadily manifested their devotion to the revolution.[13]

The first to lose their heads on the guillotine in the slaughter sanctioned by the law and the tribunals were the former queen, Marie-Antoinette, other members of the royal family, and some aristocrats. Several Girondins who had the audacity to urge the government to use caution and humanity followed, and by early 1794 the victims were coming from every social class, including the radical *sans-culottes*. Not even Danton, a member of the Committee for Public Safety, was immune; in early April he felt the executioner's blade after Robespierre decided he was not militant enough for the sake of the cause. Eventually, Robespierre's efforts to purge the government of his personal enemies went too far and he too was arrested and summarily executed. The Terror, having run its course, left in its wake a death toll of more than twenty-five thousand.

## The Rise of Napoléon

Shortly after Robespierre's death, the Revolution entered a new, generally more moderate phase known as the Thermidorian Reaction.[14] Most of the laws and tribunals of the Terror were dismantled and Girondins who had been denounced and/or imprisoned were allowed to resume their seats in the Convention. Its leaders now abandoned efforts to make France a true democracy and instead created a modified republic that was really an oligarchy (from the Greek word meaning "rule of the few"). People with a certain amount of property (and all soldiers) were allowed to vote for members of two legislative houses, the members of which then chose from their own ranks a five-man executive body, the Directory.

Although it wisely made peace with Prussia and Spain, the Directory remained at war with Austria and Britain. Partly out of necessity, therefore, the government increasingly came to rely on the power of the army rather than the broad support of the French people, which it lacked. As historian Donald Kagan points out:

> All the soldiers could vote. Moreover, within the army, created and sustained by the Revolution, stood officers who were eager for power and ambitious for political conquest. The results of the instability of the Directory and the growing role of the army held profound consequences not only for France but for the entire world.[15]

It is no exaggeration to sum up these consequences in a single name—Napoléon Bonaparte. Napoléon had become an artillery officer in 1785 and worked his way up through the ranks, becoming a general in 1793. Leading an attack on Italy aimed at depriving Austria of its support there, in 1795 he crushed two enemy armies and on his own initiative concluded a treaty with Austria, thereby taking it out of the war. Soon afterward, he brought all of Italy and Switzerland under French domination and then invaded Egypt, hoping to damage British trade and communications with northern Africa. Alarmed at these aggressions, in 1799 Britain, Austria, Russia, and Turkey formed a new anti-French coalition that threatened to bring France to its knees.

At this juncture, the wily and ambitious Napoléon took advantage of the fact that the Directory had become discredited and nearly impotent. He lent his military support to a coup engineered by himself and the writer Abbé Sieyès, by then one of the members of the Directory. The legislature was replaced with a coalition of three "consuls" (from the name of the administrator-generals of the ancient Roman Republic), one of them Napoléon; but he quickly and easily pushed the others aside and became First Consul, in essence, dictator of France. The establishment of the so-called Consulate brought the decade-long Revolution to a close. Napoléon now offered the war-weary French people security and order, and for the time being they accepted. At the time no one realized that in the next several years he would lead the nation first to glory and then to disaster in some of the bloodiest and most decisive battles Europe had ever seen.

## The Birth Struggle of Modern Europe

Thus, in a very few tumultuous years France underwent a rapid evolution from monarchy to constitutional monarchy to constitutional republic to near anarchy to oligarchy and finally to military dictatorship. In the short run the Revolution failed to make France a democracy. But in the long run it promoted the development of democracy and social reform not only in France, after Napoléon eventually fell from power, but elsewhere, because its ideas of liberty and equality lived on. For Europe and the world, writes Robert R. Palmer, one of the major modern scholars of revolutionary France, the Revolution introduced new crucial values, new status strivings, new levels of expectation. It changed the essence of the community and of the individual's sense of membership in it and his relationship to fellow citizens and fellow men. It even changed the feeling for history, or the idea of what could or ought to happen in history and in the world. . . . A whole system of civilization seemed to have fallen, and a new one to be struggling to be born.[16]

From that birth struggle eventually rose the nations of modern Europe, nearly all of which are run today by representatives of the people, not by kings or dictators. By showing that such government was possible and also decidedly preferable to the more repressive systems of the past, the French Revolution helped to transform the world.

## Notes

1. William Doyle, *The Oxford History of the French Revolution*. Oxford: Clarendon Press, 1989, p. 423.

2. George Rudé, *The French Revolution: Its Causes, Its History, and Its Legacy After 200 Years*. New York: Weidenfeld and Nicolson, 1988, pp. 1–2.

3. R.K. Gooch, *Parliamentary Government in France: Revolutionary Origins, 1789–1791*. New York: Russell and Russell, 1960, p. 15.

4. Quoted in D.I. Wright, ed., *The French Revolution: Introductory Documents*. St. Lucia: University of Queensland Press, 1974, pp. 31–32.

5. *What Is the Third Estate?* quoted in Wright, *The French Revolution*, p. 2.

6. Quoted in E.L. Higgins, ed., *The French Revolution as Told by Contemporaries*. Boston: Houghton Mifflin, 1939, p. 84.

7. *Declaration of the Rights of Man and Citizen*, quoted in Lynn Hunt, ed., *The French Revolution and Human Rights: A Brief Documentary History*. Boston: St. Martin's Press, 1996, p. 77.

8. Quoted in Higgins, *The French Revolution as Told by Contemporaries*, p. 130.

9. The name derived from the fact that at the time Dominican friars were called Jacobins, and the club held meetings in a Dominican monastery in Paris.

10. Arthur J. May, *A History of Civilization: The Mid–Seventeenth Century to Modern Times*. New York: Scribners, 1964, pp. 219–20.

11. The literal translation of the term is "without breeches," a reference to the long trousers working people wore, in contrast to the knee breeches traditionally worn by aristocrats.

12. Early in 1793, British leaders made written protest a treasonable offense and attempted to censor the press; Prussian leaders joined with the aristocracy and

Lutheran Church to stifle dissent; and in Russia, Queen Catherine burned the works of popular French philosophers, including Voltaire, and exiled freedom-minded Russian writers to Siberia.

13. Quoted in John H. Stewart, ed., *A Documentary Survey of the French Revolution.* New York: Macmillan, 1951, p. 478.

14. This term was a variation of Thermidor, the name given to the period of late July and early August in the new revolutionary calendar introduced by the Convention in September 1793; after Thermidor 9 and 10 in the year 2 (corresponding to July 27 and 28, 1794), the government's new leaders were often referred to as Thermidorians.

15. Donald Kagan et al., *The Western Heritage, 1300–1815.* New York: Macmillan, 1983, p. 672.

16. R.R. Palmer, *The Age of Democratic Revolution: The Challenge.* Princeton, NJ: Princeton University Press, 1959, p. 441.

# Chapter 1

# The Causes of the French Revolution

Turning | Points
IN WORLD HISTORY

# The Old French Social Order Made Revolution Inevitable

Arthur J. May

In this overview of sociopolitical conditions in France in the years directly preceding the French Revolution, noted historian of modern European history Arthur J. May, formerly of the University of Rochester, contrasts the nearly absolute powers of the king and the luxurious lives of the clergy and nobles with the daily deprivations of the peasants. Despite their privileges, May points out, the aristocrats, along with the members of the small moneyed middle class, had grievances with the old order, leading to discontent and a desire for change among all social classes.

France in the eighteenth century was the leading nation of Europe. Her large standing army, her excellent diplomatic service, her bureaucratic officialdom, her economic policies, her elaborate and immoral court, her ideas, manners and language were admired and imitated by other countries. Although upset by wars and recurrent famines, French standards of comfort moved modestly upward in the eighteenth century as is revealed in one way by the growth in population from about eighteen to twenty-six millions. "In spite of the abuses in administration," Frederick the Great wrote, "France is the most powerful state in Europe."

Unconventional French writers set in motion a rising tide of active discontent with prevailing institutions and customs. The growing French middle class, wealthy, intelligent, self-assertive, clamored for a share in public affairs and demanded that the special immunities and privileges of clergy

Reprinted from Arthur J. May, *A History of Civilization: The Mid-seventeenth Century to Modern Times*, 2nd ed. (New York: Scribner's, 1964).

and aristocracy should be taken away. And the social structure of eighteenth-century France typified reasonably well that of Continental Europe as a whole.

It has been said that the history of France from the death of Louis XIV to 1788 is the history of the approach of the Revolution. There is much solid truth in that judgment, but it is very easy to fall into the error of portraying a period of history in the light of what happened afterward. It is misleading, actually, to interpret French developments of the eighteenth century as pointing unerringly toward the revolutionary explosion of 1789. Few men, if indeed any, foresaw an upheaval of the kind that in fact occurred—one of the most stirring and pregnant events of all recorded history.

But an analysis of the structure of French society, the real nature of the Old Regime, discloses more than mere hints on why the Revolution came to pass.

## Clergy and Church

The social order of Continental Europe was anchored firmly on the assumption of human inequality. By reason of birth or calling, it was believed, men belonged to precise social castes in keeping with the will and the wish of the Almighty. Broadly speaking, there were two social categories: the privileged and the rest of humanity. The privileged element, in turn, was divided into the churchmen, or First Estate, and the aristocracy, the Second Estate. Considerable differences existed among the members of these groups in education, breeding, income and outlook.

The sacred nature of their vocation, coupled with long-standing tradition, placed the Christian clergy at the very top of the French social pyramid. Counting all categories, bishops and abbots, monks and nuns, parish priests and assistants, this class exceeded 130,000 on the eve of the Revolution. The higher clergy, prelates and abbots, were recruited largely from the titled aristocracy and shared the general outlook of that class; not a few of them were impregnated with the spirit of rationalism and took their ecclesiastical responsibilities lightly. Occupying luxurious palaces and recipients of fat incomes, the leading ecclesiastics belonged to the royal entourage. Many a bishop knew little about his diocese and landed estates except that they were the sources of his income.

Another story must, however, be related about the parish priests who in the main were of humble origins, as was true, also, of most monks. Living close to their parishioners, attentive to duties and morally decent, the priests were generally respected and beloved by those to whom they ministered. This was more especially the case in the rural areas. Incomes of priests were extremely modest, often they lived in want, and the sumptuous worldly way of life of their superiors generated bitter indignation. In the first flush of the Revolution the lower clergy sided decisively with the unprivileged mass of the French population.

Across the centuries, extensive properties had accumulated in the hands of churchmen. To them, or more accurately to the Catholic Church herself, belonged more than a tenth of the acreage of the kingdom as well as valuable properties in the cities and towns. In addition to revenue from these sources, the clergy collected a tithe from the faithful. Nominally a tenth of one's income, the actual amount of the tithe varied from a twelfth to a twentieth in keeping with local custom; resistance to paying the tithe mounted in the eighteenth century, producing an enormous crop of lawsuits. Church properties and churchmen were exempt from practically all direct taxes, though periodically financial grants were made to the royal treasury. . . .

## Crown and Aristocracy

The king of France, like his fellow monarchs, took precedence over all his subjects. Ruler by the sanction of the Almighty, the object of prayers by the clergy for his health and salvation, the king was accountable for his stewardship only to God. No constitution other than tradition, no national assembly defined or infringed upon his authority. All public power, executive, legislative and judicial reposed in his hands. The king ruled as well as reigned.

In the royal name laws were published, public moneys

collected and disbursed and officials appointed. The king was responsible, moreover, for diplomatic strategy and foreign policies and he was commander-in-chief of the fighting services. He possessed power to commit any man to a state prison—such as the huge, glowering Bastille in Paris—for the rest of his days without explanation or trial. Invested with immense grandeur and surrounded by pomp and pageantry, the king was looked upon as a benevolent, fatherly protector, infallible too—or so at least Frenchmen were taught and doubtless the vast majority believed. Hoary and hallowed tradition, the Christian Church and her clergy, the privileged aristocracy, the officialdom and the standing army—these were the pillars upon which the Bourbon monarchy rested.

In reality the prestige of a French monarch depended to no inconsiderable extent upon his personal qualities and character, or at any rate, upon the image which the populace had of his personality. In reality, too, public policies were determined by ministers and top-ranking bureaucrats who had access to the royal ear. The more alert of these men were not unaffected by the growing volume of criticism of the conduct of state business and of the prevailing institutions of government themselves.

The French aristocracy was composed of about 400,000 people who owned approximately a fifth of the soil of the kingdom. This estate was divided into an older element, whose ancestors had historically belonged to this caste, and men ennobled for public services or by reason of marriage or of an office they filled. About a thousand families, the élite of the élite, comprised the court aristocracy. They derived their incomes principally from great landed estates, whose management was entrusted to stewards. Properties inherited by the Marquis de Lafayette, to illustrate, yielded an income equivalent to something like $150,000 a year. Certain grandees received donations from the royal treasury or held sinecures [offices that provided revenue without work] in State or Church which paid handsomely. Even so, many an aristocrat was obliged to place mortgages on his land in order to meet debts.

The nobility of France had no direct responsibility for state affairs. In that respect the French aristocracy stood apart from the aristocracies of other countries. On the Continent nobles had been drawn into some form of public service, while in Britain they actually managed the government. And yet, although deprived of independent political authority, the French patrician class was more frequently than not the actual master of the kingdom. King and ministers repeatedly danced to the will or the whim of the more influential aristocrats.

France, very definitely, was an aristocratically ordered society. Whether at Versailles or in spacious rural chateaux, courtiers and courtesans lived a life of refined luxury, marked by conspicuous consumption in houses and furnishings, in clothes, carriages and stables, profligate frivolities and expensive entertainments. With their decorative swords, plumed hats, powdered wigs, silk stockings and suavity of manners, these proud folk formed a caste apart, a slice of Western humanity that has vanished beyond recall. The grandees had their special tastes in art and literature—some were generous patrons of the arts and sciences—and their own standards of personal behavior. . . .

As a class, nobles were exempt from most varieties of taxation and received privileged treatment in criminal trials. From the peasants they exacted rentals and other dues, which, though not large in amount, were thoroughly hated by those who paid them. Nobles maintained local courts in which extortionate fees were charged and they jealously guarded the privilege of the profitable sport of hunting. Over the Continent as a whole the aristocracy comprised a kind of international fraternity. . . .

## The Third Estate

More than twenty-four million Frenchmen, bourgeoisie, artisans, town laborers and countryfolk, were grouped in the unprivileged "Third" estate. The bourgeoisie, or propertied middle classes, had grown in response to the expansion of trade and industry and improvement in means of transportation, until it equalled the aristocracy in sheer numbers. Not at all homogeneous, this group embraced financiers, merchants, manufacturers and shipowners, shopkeepers, members of the liberal professions of law and medicine, writers and journalists and skilled craftsmen. Prosperous middle class families owned about a sixth of the land of the kingdom.

French trade multiplied fourfold in the course of the eighteenth century and the bourgeoisie benefited greatly. Some large fortunes were piled up by businessmen and by moneylenders who extended loans to the straitened government, or cashed in on advances to the nobility. In this category, too, were financiers who purchased the right of gathering the indirect taxes in sections of the kingdom and pocketed the excess that was collected. Manufacturing of course was carried on principally under guild roofs, but some enterprising individuals had accumulated wealth from the domestic or putting-out type of production. By 1789 a few rich capitalists were operating large-scale textile factories and iron mills. The professional classes, lawyers most of all, had increased in numbers and in prosperity. . . .

By and large . . . the bourgeoisie hotly resented their inferior social status. . . . They longed for an order of society in which money, not birth, would be the controlling consideration. They desired greater scope for personal initiative and enterprise, the elimination of state interference with the free play of economic forces. They were keenly interested in attaining a fuller measure of happiness on this earth.

Ambitious, hard-working, self-assured, the French bourgeoisie greedily devoured the publications of the *philosophes* which so engagingly expressed what the middle classes thought. Books forbidden by the censorship were "bootlegged" about with remarkable abandon, and their contents were discussed in homes, societies, clubs and lodges. Men of the middle classes came confidently to believe that the future belonged to them. The French Revolution would be a bourgeois movement in the main; and the minds and emotions of the middle classes were prepared for significant changes before they made them the work of their hands.

Paris and a dozen other substantial cities contained a propertyless working class. There were guildsmen, for instance, who expected to rise to master rank, shop and factory employees, unskilled day laborers and peasants driven from the land by harsh conditions or piecing out their incomes by seasonal employment. No organizations or clear feeling of class consciousness united these wage workers. Of the Paris population, which exceeded 500,000, approximately half belonged to wage-earning families. Wholly untaught, poorly fed, poorly housed, poorly clothed, working long hours for small pay, this miserable element readily responded to ideological fashions and one-word arguments. Cruel want goaded lowly Parisians to street riots on several occasions in the eighteenth century, though they were in fact less unruly than their counterparts in London.

## The Peasantry

Nine out of ten Frenchmen depended upon the land for their daily bread. Probably somewhere between two-fifths and one-half of the land of the kingdom belonged to peasants, in the sense that they could not be dispossessed and could bequeath holdings to heirs. For a good deal of the land which they worked, peasants owed nominal rentals to nobles in the neighborhood. Most of the rustics operated only small farms, sufficient merely to supply the necessities of their personal families, if indeed that. . . . Still other peasants cultivated land on shares or hired out as day laborers. Underemployment was a chronic evil in rural France. When crop yields were short, many poor peasants were reduced to beggary or actually starved, and insufficiency of food was commonplace.

Acute distress in the countryside fanned discontent and encouraged vagabondage and thievery. . . .

A large growth of rural population in the eighteenth century worsened the material lot of the French peasantry. Farm animals were scarce, and manure, consequently, was in limited supply, a handicap to more intensive cultivation. French agriculture failed to satisfy the food requirements of the growing urban population.

Apart from rentals to landlords, the peasants had to make payments for the use of the manor grain-mill and wine press.

They deeply resented regulations which reserved the snaring of game to the nobility, and made it a crime to kill animals that invaded their growing crops. And many deliberately tried to evade their obligation to the church, the tithe. Far more burdensome than the dues owed to lords or to the Lord were the taxes and other obligations paid to the rapacious Bourbon government. The basic direct tax was the *taille* levied on real property or, in places on crops, and varying considerably in amount in different sections of the kingdom. Assessments were increased if a cottage was fixed up or fields kept in good condition, so calculating peasants tended to neglect their properties. Payment of this *taille* was a mark of inferiority for the upper classes were exempt.

Other direct taxes were the *twentieth*, which sometimes ran as high as a sixth of one's income and a poll tax paid by the head of every household. In effect, a tax was the *corvée*, which compelled peasants to perform unremunerated labor to keep roadways in trim or to mend bridges and canals. They might be called upon, too, for carts to move troops or to provide lodgings for soldiers. Lucky they were if they escaped enrollment in the royal army. . . .

Counting everything, at least three-fifths, probably more, of the income of the poor man was drained off by clergy, nobility and state, so that the peasants though mostly freemen were economically enchained. It was the Bourbon government that was the insatiable Leviathan and the rustics hated and cursed it with primitive fervor. Nothing so feeds revolutionary ardor as a deep sense of grievance. . . .

This sweeping survey throws into bold relief the actualities, the inequalities, the archaicisms of Old World society in the eighteenth century. And it must be emphasized that the lot of the non-privileged in France was superior to that anywhere else in Europe. Because there was more wealth, more enlightenment in France, Frenchmen were more dynamically discontented with the status quo, more ready for drastic changes.

# Major Causes of the Revolution

E.J. Hobsbawm

In this analysis of the factors leading up to the outbreak of the French Revolution, historian E.J. Hobsbawm, formerly of King's College and London University, mentions the monarchy's financial debt, the rising power of the bourgeoisie (middle class), and the influence of liberal philosophers on the bourgeoisie. Hobsbawm places most of his emphasis, however, on the aristocrats' attempt to regain economic and political powers lost over the course of the eighteenth century. Part of this attempt, he says, was a "feudal reaction," a tightening of the aristocracy's grip on the peasants. But the nobles underestimated the determination and powerful political potential of the third estate, which finally stood up for its own rights.

The French Revolution . . . remains *the* revolution of its time, and not merely one, though the most prominent, of its kind. And its origins must therefore be sought not merely in the general conditions of Europe, but in the specific situation of France. Its peculiarity is perhaps best illustrated in international terms. Throughout the eighteenth century France was the major international economic rival of Britain. Her foreign trade, which multiplied fourfold between 1720 and 1780, caused anxiety; her colonial system was in certain areas (such as the West Indies) more dynamic than the British. Yet France was not a power like Britain, whose foreign policy was already determined substantially by the interests of capitalist expansion. She was the most powerful and in many ways the most typical of the old aris-

Reprinted from E.J. Hobsbawm, *The Age of Revolution* (London: Weidenfeld & Nicolson, 1962) by permission of Orion Publishing Group, London.

tocratic absolute monarchies of Europe. In other words, the conflict between the official framework and the vested interests of the old régime and the rising new social forces was more acute in France than elsewhere.

The new forces knew fairly precisely what they wanted. Turgot, the [French] economist, stood for an efficient exploitation of the land, for free enterprise and trade, for a standardized, efficient administration of a single homogeneous national territory, and the abolition of all restrictions and social inequalities which stood in the way of the development of national resources and rational, equitable administration and taxation. Yet his attempt to apply such a programme as the first minister of Louis XVI in 1774–76 failed lamentably, and the failure is characteristic. Reforms of this character, in modest doses, were not incompatible with or unwelcome to absolute monarchies. On the contrary, since they strengthened their hand, they were . . . widely propagated at this time among the so-called 'enlightened despots'. But in most of the countries of 'enlightened despotism' such reforms were either inapplicable, and therefore mere theoretical flourishes, or unlikely to change the general character of their political and social structure; or else they failed in the face of the resistance of the local aristocracies and other vested interests, leaving the country to relapse into a somewhat tidied-up version of its former state. In France they failed more rapidly than elsewhere, for the resistance of the vested interests was more effective. But the results of this failure were more catastrophic for the monarchy; and the forces of bourgeois change were far too strong to relapse into inactivity. They merely transformed their hopes from an enlightened monarchy to the people or 'the nation'.

## The Feudal Reaction

Nevertheless, such a generalisation does not take us far towards an understanding of why the revolution broke out when it did, and why it took the remarkable road it did. For this it is most useful to consider the so-called 'feudal reaction' which actually provided the spark to explode the powder-barrel of France.

The 400,000 or so persons who, among the twenty-three million Frenchmen, formed the nobility, the unquestioned 'first order' of the nation, though not so absolutely safeguarded against the intrusion of lesser orders as in Prussia and elsewhere, were secure enough. They enjoyed considerable privileges, including exemption from several taxes (but not from as many as the better-organized clergy), and the

## The Arrogant and Superficial Nobles

*In these brief excerpts from her recollections of the Revolution, Madame de Staël, daughter of the popular finance minister Jacques Necker, cites the arrogance, superficiality, and ineptitude of the French nobles as a factor in their downfall and the rise of the common people.*

The party of the aristocrats, that is to say, the privileged, are persuaded that a king of firmer character would have been able to prevent the Revolution. They forget that they themselves were the first to begin, courageously and rightly, the attack upon the royal power; and what resistance could this power oppose to them, since the nation was then on their side? Ought they to complain of having been the stronger against the king and the weaker against the people? That was inevitable. . . .

The great nobles of France were not very well informed, because they had nothing to gain by being so. Grace in conversation, which would please at court, was the surest means of arriving at honors. This superficial education was one cause of the downfall of the nobles: they could no longer fight against the intelligence of the third estate; they should have tried to surpass it. The great lords would have by degrees gained supremacy in the primary assemblies through their knowledge of administration, as formerly they had acquired it by their swords; and the public mind would have been prepared for the establishment of free institutions in France.

Quoted in E.L. Higgins, ed., *The French Revolution as Told by Contemporaries.* Boston: Houghton Mifflin, 1939, p. 20.

right to receive feudal dues. Politically their situation was less brilliant. Absolute monarchy, while entirely aristocratic and even feudal in its *ethos* [character], had deprived the nobles of political independence and responsibility and cut down their old representative institutions—estates and *parlements*—so far as possible. The fact continued to rankle among the higher aristocracy. . . . Economically the nobles' worries were by no means negligible. Fighters rather than earners by birth and tradition—nobles were even formally debarred from exercising a trade or profession—they depended on the income of their estates, or, if they belonged to the favoured minority of large or court nobles, on wealthy marriages, court pensions, gifts and sinecures. But the expenses of noble status were large and rising, their incomes—since they were rarely businesslike managers of their wealth, if they managed it at all—fell. Inflation tended to reduce the value of fixed revenues such as rents.

It was therefore natural that the nobles should use their one main asset, the acknowledged privileges of the order. Throughout the eighteenth century, in France as in many other countries, they encroached steadily upon the official posts which the absolute monarchy had preferred to fill with technically competent and politically harmless middle class men. . . . Consequently the nobility not merely exasperated the feelings of the middle class by their successful competition for official posts; they also undermined the state itself by an increasing tendency to take over provincial and central administration. Similarly they—and especially the poorer provincial gentlemen who had few other resources—attempted to counteract the decline in their income by squeezing the utmost out of their very considerable feudal rights to exact money (or more rarely service) from the peasantry. An entire profession, the *feudists*, came into existence to revive obsolete rights of this kind or to maximize the yield of existing ones. . . . Consequently the nobility exasperated not only the middle class but also the peasantry.

The position of this vast class, comprising perhaps 80 per cent of all Frenchmen, was far from brilliant. They were indeed in general free, and often landowners. In actual quantity noble estates covered only one-fifth of the land, clerical estates perhaps another 6 per cent with regional variations. Thus in the diocese of Montpellier the peasants already owned 38 to 40 per cent of the land, the bourgeoisie 18 to 19, the nobles 15 to 16, the clergy 3 to 4, while one-fifth was common land. In fact, however, the great majority were landless or with insufficient holdings, a deficiency increased by the prevailing technical backwardness; and the general land-hunger was intensified by the rise in population. Feudal dues, tithes and taxes took a large and rising proportion of the peasant's income, and inflation reduced the value of the remainder. For only the minority of peasants who had a constant surplus for sale benefited from the rising prices; the rest, in one way or another, suffered from them, especially in times of bad harvest, when famine prices ruled. There is little doubt that in the twenty years preceding the Revolution the situation of the peasants grew worse for these reasons.

## The Aristocrats Exploit the Crisis

The financial troubles of the monarchy brought matters to a head. The administrative and fiscal structure of the kingdom was grossly obsolete, and . . . the attempt to remedy this by the reforms of 1774–76 failed, defeated by the resistance of vested interests headed by the *parlements*. . . . Various expedients were tried with diminishing success, but nothing short of a fundamental reform, which mobilized the real and considerable taxable capacity of the country could cope with a situation in which expenditure outran revenue by at least 20 per cent, and no effective economies were possible. For though the extravagance of [the royal court at] Versailles has often been blamed for the crisis, court expenditure only amounted to 6 per cent of the total in 1788. War, navy and diplomacy made up one-quarter, the service of [interest on] the existing debt one-half. War and debt . . . broke the back of the monarchy.

The government's crisis gave the aristocracy and the *parlements* their chance. They refused to pay without an extension of their privileges. The first breach in the front of absolutism was a hand-picked but nevertheless rebellious 'assembly of notables' called in 1787 to grant the government's demands. The second, and decisive, was the desperate decision to call the States-General—the old feudal assembly of the realm, buried since 1614. The Revolution thus began as an aristocratic attempt to recapture the state. This attempt miscalculated for two reasons: it underestimated the independent intentions of the 'Third Estate'—the fictional entity deemed to represent all who were neither nobles nor clergy, but in fact dominated by the middle class—and it overlooked the profound economic and social crisis into which it threw its political demands.

The French Revolution was not made or led by a formed party or movement in the modern sense, nor by men attempting to carry out a systematic programme. It hardly even threw up 'leaders' of the kind to which twentieth century revolutions have accustomed us, until the post-revolutionary figure of Napoleon. Nevertheless a striking consensus of general ideas among a fairly coherent social group gave the revolutionary movement effective unity. The group was the 'bourgeoisie'; its ideas were those of classical liberalism, as formulated by the 'philosophers'. . . . To this extent 'the philosophers' can be justly made responsible for the Revolution. It would have occurred without them; but they probably made the difference between a mere breakdown of an old régime and the effective and rapid substitution of a new one.

# The Monarchy's Financial Crisis

William Doyle

William Doyle, chairman of the School of History at the University of Bristol in England and a respected scholar of the French Revolution, here focuses on one of the Revolution's chief causative factors—the steadily worsening state of the royal finances in the 1770s and 1780s. According to Doyle, when, in November 1783, Louis XVI appointed former provincial administrator Charles Alexander Calonne as comptroller-general, the dominant minister of state, Calonne found that he had very limited options for a strictly financial solution. This finally led Calonne to conclude that the nation could only be saved from bankruptcy and ruin by a drastic reform of the whole governmental system.

The revolution that was to sweep away the political institutions of old France, and shake her society to its foundations, did not begin on 14 July 1789. By that time the old order was already in ruins, beyond reconstruction. This was the result of a chain of events that can be traced as far back as 20 August 1786. For it was on that day that Calonne, comptroller-general of the royal finances, first came to Louis XVI and informed him that the state was on the brink of financial collapse.

We have no absolutely reliable or completely unambiguous figures to illustrate the financial condition of France in 1786. Nor did contemporaries have such figures. Even Calonne, with all the accounts of the royal treasury at his disposal, claimed that it had taken him two years to arrive at his own assessment of the problem. But the seriousness of the

Reprinted from William Doyle, *Origins of the French Revolution*, ©William Doyle, 1980, 1988, by permission of Oxford University Press.

situation was beyond dispute. According to Calonne, the total revenue for 1786 would amount to 475 million *livres*, but expenditure would probably total 587 millions—a deficit of 112 millions, or almost a quarter of the annual revenue. When Louis XVI had come to the throne in 1774, Calonne claimed, the deficit had been 40 millions, and it had even fallen over the next two years. But since 1777 it had risen steadily, and there was every prospect, over the next few years, of its rising further if drastic action was not soon taken. The basic reason for this deterioration was that since 1777 there had been an enormous rise in state borrowing and consequently in the annual interest and repayments that the treasury was obliged to disburse. Since 1776, Calonne claimed, 1,250 millions had been borrowed. Until 1794, 50 millions per year of short-term loans would fall due for repayment, and meanwhile, the cost of servicing the total debt ate up nearly half of the annual revenue. Worse still, no less than 280 millions of the next year's revenues had already been anticipated in order to raise money for earlier expenditure.

Financial difficulties were nothing new under the French monarchy. Indeed, throughout the seventeenth and eighteenth centuries they were the normal state of affairs; it was the rare moments of financial health that were extraordinary. Nor was the cause of these difficulties any mystery. Successive kings had always spent too much on war. The wars of Louis XIV had imposed a crippling legacy of debt on the royal finances, and although this burden was much alleviated by the great financial crash of 1720–21, which enabled the government to write off huge sums, four major European and overseas wars since that time had brought matters once more to crisis proportions. They were already serious by 1763, at the end of seven years of costly and unsuccessful conflict on a worldwide scale; the deficit had reached 50 millions, and for the next fifteen years successive comptrollers-general of the finances warned unceasingly against the dangers of further wars. French participation in the American War of Independence between 1778 and 1783 was glorious and successful, but it confirmed these ministers' worst fears. By 1783, the financial situation was as bad as it had been in

1715, and over the next three years it continued to deteriorate to the point which Calonne announced to the king in August 1786.

## Possible Remedies?

A number of obvious expedients are open to governments in financial difficulties. Unfortunately, most of these expedients were not open to Calonne—or, if they were, there were reasons why they could not prove as effective as they should.

One natural step, for example, was to effect economies [i.e., reduce spending]. There was undoubtedly scope for this, and the plan which Calonne put forward to the Assembly of Notables the next year was to include a number of money-saving proposals. Nevertheless, none of the major items of public expenditure could be substantially reduced. . . . The armed forces could only be markedly reduced at the cost of jeopardizing France's international position at a moment when the internal instability of the Dutch Republic and uncertainties in Eastern Europe following the death of Frederick the Great made the international situation ominous. Economies, therefore, must largely be a matter of trimming expenditure over a whole range of minor items such as pensions, the royal household, public works, and welfare services which together accounted for only about one-seventh of annual outlay . . . nowhere near enough to meet a deficit on the scale of 1786. Clearly economies could only be effective in conjunction with more comprehensive measures.

A second possibility would be to increase taxes. Yet France was already one of the most highly taxed nations in Europe. It is true that the average Dutchman or Englishman paid more per head in taxes than his French counterpart; but in France there were immense regional diversities, so that taxpayers in the Paris region paid more per head than anybody else in Europe. And when we consider that the populations of Great Britain and the Dutch Republic were in any case far wealthier as a whole than that of France, the French burden appears all the greater. What is more, it seemed to have increased inordinately within living memory. . . . In 1749, a new tax on landed property of 5 per cent had been introduced—the *vingtième*. It proved to be permanent. In 1756, it had been doubled for a limited period, but in practice the government never felt able to do without the extra revenue, so this second *vingtième* became in effect as permanent as the first. Between 1760 and 1763, the most costly period of the Seven Years War, a third *vingtième* was levied; and in 1783, it was reintroduced with the assurance that it would end three years after peace was concluded. That moment came at the end of 1786, and this imminent fall in revenue was another of the factors which led Calonne to confront the crisis when he did. . . .

Another possibility was for the state simply to renounce its overwhelming burden of debt by declaring bankruptcy. Earlier governments had often adopted this expedient; but over the eighteenth century it had come to seem less and less respectable. The financial crash of 1720, in which thousands of government creditors were ruined, and a series of reductions in the *rentes* (government annuities) in the chaotic years following that crisis, had instilled French public opinion with a deep hostility to breaches of public faith, and from 1726 onwards governments had striven to keep public confidence by avoiding any suggestion that they might default on their debts. . . . The lesson seemed clear; bankruptcy was not only dishonourable, it destroyed the state's credit and made further borrowing difficult. . . . Turgot, and every minister who followed him, Calonne included, set their faces firmly against even partial bankruptcy. The determination of successive revolutionary assemblies down to 1797 to honour the debts accumulated under the old order shows how deeply and generally public opinion shared the view that the public debt should be sacrosanct.

But Calonne could hardly go on borrowing. It is true that the plan of action which he laid before the king contained proposals for further loans in order to cover the repayments of the coming years, but there was no long-term future in fighting a debt problem by new borrowings. In any case it was uncertain whether such borrowing would even be possible. The French government already borrowed money on terms distinctly less favourable than either the British or the

Dutch, because in France there was no publicly supported bank through which government credit could be cheaply channelled. . . . In the absence of a bank, the government was compelled to rely on intermediaries for raising its loans, bodies like the municipality of Paris, the estates of provinces that retained them (like Languedoc and Brittany), or great corporations like the clergy, all of which could borrow money on better terms than the king. But when needs were extraordinary even these resources were not enough. Then, the government was compelled to float loans on its own behalf, but on terms so generous that even the most prudent investor found them hard to resist. This is what happened between 1777 and 1786. . . .

An expedient that Calonne did not consider was a reform of the system by which the government financed its activities. One reason why it took him so long to come to any conclusions about the true state of the finances was that the king had no central treasury where accounts were kept, revenues taken in, and payments made. Nor was there any real notion of an annual budget. Most of the state's finances were handled by independent financiers who had bought the right to handle government revenues, either through membership of the company of Farmers-General, who collected most of the indirect taxes, or through buying an office of accountant (variously called payers, receivers, or treasurers) to a government department. Once in office, all that these officials were obliged to do was to receive or pay out funds on the government's orders, and send in periodic accounts to the crown's courts of audit, the *chambres des comptes*. What they did with the money in their accounts otherwise was their own affair. And what they often did with it in practice was to lend it to the government in short-term credits—so that the king found himself borrowing and paying interest on his own money. The day-to-day payments of the government, in fact, depended on short-term credits of this sort, the *anticipations* which ate up so much of the expected revenue for 1787, advanced by men who were nominally state employees, but who in reality were private businessmen making a profit from manipulating public funds. Nor did such businessmen confine their activities to juggling with the state's money. They normally had extensive private financial dealings, too, and made no distinction between the two fields of activity. So that when, in times of economic stringency, their operations came under strain, so did the finances of the government. This is what happened in 1770 and again in 1786–87, when the government's difficulties were heralded by the bank-ruptcy of a number of its financiers. A state bank would, of course, have freed the government from its dependence on these profiteering agents, who constituted in effect a body of several hundred petty bankers. . . .

## The Call for Comprehensive Reform

With so many courses of action either closed or considered impractical, what then did Calonne propose to do in order to resolve the crisis? Nothing could put it more clearly than his own words. 'I shall easily show,' he declared to the king, 'that it is impossible to tax further, ruinous to be always bor-rowing and not enough to confine ourselves to economical reforms and that, with matters as they are, ordinary ways being unable to lead us to our goal, the only effective rem-edy, the only course left to take, the only means of manag-ing finally to put the finances truly in order, must consist in revivifying the entire State by recasting all that is vicious in its constitution.' He was proposing something quite un-precedented in the history of the monarchy—a total and comprehensive reform of all its institutions, according to clear principles, in such a way that it should never fall into difficulties like those of the 1780s again.

In the document he presented to the king, *Summary of a Plan for the Improvement of the Finances*, Calonne never de-fined his guiding principle in a few words. But it emerged very clearly from the way he put the problem. . . . In short, the French state lacked rational organization and uniform principles, and it was not enough to attempt to solve finan-cial problems, as previous ministries had, by exclusively fi-nancial means. Calonne believed that it was now necessary to reform the economy, government, and to some degree French society itself.

# France's Weak and Frivolous Ruling Couple

Olivier Bernier

In this brief but informative sketch, Olivier Bernier, a leading authority on the French Revolution and acclaimed lecturer at the Metropolitan Museum of Art, reveals the numerous character flaws and deficiencies of Louis XVI and his wife, Marie Antoinette. Unfortunately for France, at a time when it desperately needed strong, selfless leadership, a weak, stubborn man and an arrogant, self-indulgent woman sat on the throne.

In 1770, France had celebrated the marriage of the sixteen-year-old heir to the throne and the fifteen-year-old Marie Antoinette, Archduchess of Austria. Although this was a purely political union meant to reaffirm the strength of the alliance between the two monarchies, the young couple soon became a symbol of hope and renewal. The Dauphin and Dauphine, indeed, seemed to embody everything for which the French yearned: they were young, virtuous, a couple in love who provided the strongest contrast to the corruption of the court. They were also the future King and Queen of France, so when they made their official entry into Paris in 1772, the capital gave them their first taste of popularity. As their carriage crossed the city, it was surrounded by huge, cheering crowds. When, in 1774, the new King and Queen, fleeing the risk of smallpox, from which Louis XV had just died, moved to La Muette, at the edge of the city, they were again able to see and hear for themselves the love their people bore them. Never, observers noted, had monarchs been so popular: here, clearly, was the start of a golden era.

Indeed, the press could not find enough compliments for them. Louis XVI, the papers said, was young but serious, caring, and virtuous; Marie Antoinette was not only beautiful but kind and compassionate; together they would rule, gently and fairly, so as to bring forth an age of peace, prosperity, and progress; and the French agreed wholeheartedly with the press. Every time the new monarchs appeared in public, they received the most rapturous of greetings. No reign, people agreed, had begun better.

## The Charm of Youth

When her husband succeeded to the throne in May 1774, Marie Antoinette, Archduchess of Austria and Queen of France, looked like a dream come true. Tall, slender, graceful, she was seductive without being really pretty; but even if her eyes were too small and her Habsburg lip too pronounced, she made up for it with a perfect complexion, a charming smile, and a shapely figure—small waist, generous bosom—shown off to advantage by the current fashions. She walked beautifully, apparently floating over the slippery parquet floors of Versailles. . . . She was famous for her grand, sweeping curtsey. Above all, at nineteen, she had the charm of youth. . . .

Of course, charm was a great quality in a new sovereign; but there was more to Marie Antoinette than that. She was known to be strictly virtuous, a refreshing quality after the late King's succession of official mistresses. She was obviously in love with her husband, and people sighed with delight as they watched the young couple strolling arm in arm. She was also close to her new family and dined several times a week with her two brothers- and sisters-in-law. She was even fond of the aunts, the sour, old-maid daughters of Louis XV; and she was widely rumored to be kindness itself. . . .

Louis XVI, too, seemed the very pattern of a good king. He had simple tastes, disliked luxury, and had no mistresses. In sharp contrast to Louis XV, his grandfather, he was faithful to his wife. He expressed the best of intentions: his first duty, he said, was to his people; and he earned himself immense popularity, right at the start of his reign, by dismissing Louis XV's hated ministers. . . . He was, unfortunately, shy and awkward, but already, under his wife's influence, he had improved noticeably. Now, with the assurance of power, he was sure to outgrow these youthful shortcomings. Finally, he was notoriously and strictly pious, and seemed therefore likely to curb the corruption all too prevalent in the Church. All in all, it was no wonder the people loved him.

## "We Are Too Young to Reign"

Unfortunately, these golden appearances were just that: to the few people who knew the young couple well, the future seemed very much less promising. It was true, for instance, that Louis had no mistresses; but then again, he was no husband. When, after much delay and hesitation, he tried to consummate his marriage, he utterly and repeatedly failed to do so. Of course, the court knew it and made fun of him, while all the way across Europe, in Vienna, the Empress

---

### A Ruler Lacking Strength of Character

*In these excerpts, France's king and queen are described by two who knew them, Marie by Baron Besenval, a Swiss army officer serving at the French court, and Louis by Madame Roland, wife of a leading Girondin.*

The queen is far from lacking intellect, but her education has been negative as far as instruction is concerned. Except for novels, she has never opened a book, and does not even seek the ideas that society can give; as soon as a subject takes a serious turn, a look of boredom comes over her face and chills the conversation. Her conversation is desultory, intermittent, and flutters from object to object. Being without natural gaiety, she amuses herself with the day's idle story, with little liberties cleverly toned down, and above all with the scandal that is found at court; that is what pleases her. Accommodating, unexacting, but without depth of feeling . . . she knew . . . nothing of friendship. . . .

Louis XVI was . . . neither the stupid imbecile that they presented for the disdain of the people, nor the fine, judicious, vir-

Maria Theresa watched with anguish—the marriage was the visible manifestation of the Franco-Austrian alliance—and wrote her daughter letter after letter asking whether there had been any change.

Sadly, the King's impotence seemed all too emblematic of his personality. At twenty, Louis XVI was immensely strong, but already running to fat, and desperately awkward. Naturally shy and uncertain, he seemed even more doltlike because he was so shortsighted as to be almost blind without the glasses he refused to wear. Worse, although not unintelligent, he seemed unable to think for himself; but if he was easily influenced, he was also capable of the most mulish obstinacy, especially when he had at last reached the wrong decision. . . .

At first, even this lack of savoir faire seemed like a good quality. The court, thundering across the Palace after Louis XV's death to pay homage to the new sovereigns, had found

tuous man that his friends described. Nature had made him an ordinary man, who would have done well in some obscure station. He was ruined in being educated for the throne, and lost through mediocrity in a difficult period when he could have been saved only through genuis and strength. An ordinary mind, brought up near the throne and taught from infancy to dissemble, acquires many advantages for dealing with people; the art of letting each see only what is suitable for him to see is for it only a habit to which practice gives an appearance of cleverness: one would have to be an idiot to appear stupid in such a situation. . . . But Louis XVI, without elevation of soul, without boldness of mind, without strength of character, still had his ideas narrowed and his sentiments perverted, so to say, by religious prejudices. . . . If he had been born two centuries earlier, and if he had had a reasonable wife, he would have made no more noise in the world than many other princes of his race who have passed across the stage without having done much good or much harm.

Quoted in E.L. Higgins, ed., *The French Revolution as Told by Contemporaries.* Boston: Houghton Mifflin, 1939, pp. 12–14.

them, embracing and kneeling, their faces awash with tears; and just as the doors opened, they were heard to say: "Protect us, O God, we are too young to reign." For once, they were right, and they proved it immediately.

Dismissing the late King's ministers—Marie Antoinette insisted on it—was no doubt popular; it was also a serious mistake. Indeed, the seeds of the Revolution were sown on that day. Because, by 1770, the ancien régime had become paralyzed by its beneficiaries' greed, Louis XV had . . . begun to modify the tax system so as to shift its burden from the poor to the rich. Unfortunately, the poor had no voice, while the rich were very well able to make themselves heard, so these changes were greeted with a chorus of disapproval; hence the paradox. The very act which earned the new King such popularity also prevented the regime from reforming itself: from that day in May 1774 Louis XVI was hostage to the most reactionary [traditional and conservative] elements in France.

## Indulging the Queen

Almost worse, he had acted against his own preference, and given in to his wife, thus setting a dangerous precedent. As for Marie Antoinette, she wanted the ministers dismissed, not because she disliked their policies, but because she thought them friends of Mme du Barry, Louis XV's mistress, against whom she bore a grudge. Thus the most basic of political decisions was made because of one of the Queen's whims, a fact not overlooked by the courtiers. "I can clearly see," Joseph II [emperor of Austria and Marie Antionette's brother] wrote in 1777, "that all the detail which is connected to personal intrigues is taken care of with the greatest attention and interest, while the essential business of the state is neglected."

In fact, Louis's impotence, as well as the slowness of his mind, made him into his wife's permanent victim. Devoured by guilt at his failure to consummate the marriage, he made up for it by indulging the sexually deprived Queen in other ways; and because, in any event, he was easy to influence, it was obvious that the person closest to him would also be the actual ruler.

Much to her mother's distress, however, Marie Antoinette usually did not choose to exert her power, at least not in the early part of the reign. For a few weeks, Maria Theresa had hoped to run the French government from Vienna, via the Austrian ambassador at Versailles and her daughter; but she quickly realized that the Queen was far too frivolous, far too easily bored and averse to hard work ever to have more than episodic influence.

Unfortunately, Marie Antoinette's thirst for amusement was coupled with a deep reluctance to do her duty. It must, in all fairness, be said that standing for hours, wearing an immensely heavy costume, while unknown ladies pass before you curtseying and kissing your hand, is not particularly entertaining; that receiving ambassadors to whom one has nothing to say is a strain; and that having dinner alone in front of a staring crowd does not make for a pleasant meal; but those were the duties of a Queen of France. Even at Versailles, monarchs had obligations as well as rights. Yet this was a situation Marie Antoinette chose to ignore. To her, being Queen meant having fun; and if that entailed canceling receptions or retreating to her private apartments, then she did just that. . . .

Far worse, it soon became clear that although Louis XVI had given his wife an allowance double that of the last Queen, she was in debt. This was partly because she became obsessed with fashion, spending the equivalent of some two million dollars a year for her clothes by 1777; partly because, although she had the crown jewels at her disposal, she kept buying diamonds; and partly because she gambled frequently and recklessly, often losing the equivalent of hundreds of thousands of dollars at cards in a single night.

All these shortcomings evoked wails from Vienna. Maria Theresa, the greatest as well as the most popular of all the Habsburgs, was a hard-working, intelligent woman who saw all too clearly that her daughter could not afford this kind of self-indulgence. Displaying yet another unappealing side of her character, Marie Antoinette took to denying the truth, to her mother and others, in order not to give up anything that amused or pleased her.

## From Unpopularity to Outright Hatred

Upsetting the Empress was perhaps not very grave; far more unfortunate, the Queen's own subjects soon got to know her better. It was true, for instance, that she was compassionate when someone suffered visibly; but it was her duty, not just to be kind to her servants but also to be charitable to the poor and sick in general. That, however, bored her; and because she was constantly in debt, she was unable to contribute financially to the various institutions that expected her patronage.

Again, her famous charm seemed to operate best at close quarters. What most people saw, however, was pride and selfishness. That the Habsburgs were superior to everyone else on earth was something Marie Antoinette never doubted. . . . As for the haughtiness of her demeanor, that was visible to all. Once, in answer to a compliment from Mme Vigée-Lebrun, who had just told her that she held her head beautifully, Marie Antoinette said: "Yes, but if I were not Queen, they would say I was arrogant, wouldn't they?" She was Queen, but they said it anyway.

And there were graver matters. . . . It had been a tradition in France, since time immemorial, that queens did not own real property; but when, in 1774, Louis XVI gave her the Petit Trianon [a small royal mansion at Versailles] and its gardens, Marie Antoinette had it enclosed with railings and gates so as to keep the public out (they were allowed throughout the great park of Versailles) and had rules posted in her own name instead of the King's. When, after that, she had a little theater built and had the gardens completely redesigned in the new English fashion, complete with lake, river, temple of Love, and village, all at great expense, unpopularity turned to outright hatred. So convinced were the people that all the state's money was going to the Queen that, in 1789, many of the Deputies to the Estates General asked to see the well-known—and wholly fictitious—room at the Trianon that had walls covered with emeralds and diamonds.

# Intellectual Contributions to the Revolution

John H. Stewart

This concise essay by the late distinguished scholar John H. Stewart, former professor of history at Case Western Reserve University, summarizes the main ideas of the scientists, philosophers, economists, and other thinkers of the Age of Enlightenment, whose works provided the intellectual background of the French Revolution. Stewart also explains the means by which these ideas reached the members of various classes and social groups.

In the realm of cultural development the eighteenth century is generally known as the Age of the Enlightenment or the Age of Reason. The former title suggests the intellectual quickening which distinguished the era; the latter designation expresses succinctly the dominant point of view of the progressive thinkers of the time. It was a period when men stressed reason as a guide to the solution of the problems of the universe and of man, an attitude of which the origin is to be found chiefly in the works of two luminaries of the previous century, Isaac Newton and John Locke.

Isaac Newton (1642–1727) was an English scientist who followed Copernicus, Galileo, and others in emancipating men from the dead hand of medieval supernaturalism and in introducing them to the study of nature. This he did in two ways. First, in his *Principia mathematica* (1687) he confirmed a growing belief in the existence of "natural laws," constant mathematical principles which determine the functioning of the universe. Second, in his emphasis on the experimental method he made it possible for the average man to come

Reprinted by permission of Prentice-Hall, Inc., Upper Saddle River, N.J., from *A Documentary Survey of the French Revolution*, by John H. Stewart, ©The Macmillan Company, 1951.

into intimate contact with nature, and to some extent to govern her actions and discover her secrets. John Locke (1632–1704), also an Englishman, was a philosopher. Like Newton he furthered the process of emancipating mankind, but in a somewhat different manner. In his *Essay concerning the Human Understanding* (1690) Locke claimed that man's mind at birth was a blank form, the ultimate patterns on which were shaped by environment and by the use of the reasoning power—in contradiction of the hitherto accepted belief in innate ideas and divine revelation. In his *Of Civil Government* (published in the same year), he provided not only a justification of the English revolutions of his own time, but a political ideology for posterity. His political philosophy affirmed that since all members of a society cannot govern, government must be delegated to a few; and that relations between governors and governed are established in some form of compact or contract involving mutual benefits and guarantees and punishments for infractions by either party to the agreement.

## A Philosophy of Natural Rights

To the thinking people of the eighteenth century the ideas of Newton and Locke assumed a special significance. The experimental method in science brought man closer to nature than ever before. Could he not, therefore, learn more of her secrets, determine additional natural laws, regulate his environment, and ultimately bring mankind into harmony with the universe—all by the use of his reasoning power? If this were true, could he not perhaps discover natural laws governing man as well as the universe, regulate his actions rationally, and bring himself into harmony with his fellow men? Such a prospect afforded an optimistic naturalism and an appreciation of life "here," in contrast with the pessimistic supernaturalism and anticipation of the life "hereafter" which had dominated the past. This somewhat distorted interpretation of profundities derived from the needs of the middle class which found, or thought it found, in these ideas a means of escape from oppression, a justification of its demand for recognition, a philosophy of "natural rights." And it is France, where the middle class was most numerous, most prosperous, and most desirous of change that affords the most notable example of the direction and diffusion of these principles by a group of thinkers usually referred to as the *philosophes*.

The most famous, and perhaps the most influential, of the *philosophes* was François Marie Arouet, commonly called Voltaire (1694–1778). Voltaire established himself as a popularizer of what he conceived to be the ideas of Newton, and as an aggressive defender of truth and tolerance. The particular object of his ridicule was the Church. He believed that the Church as an organization in eighteenth-century France was far removed from the ideas propounded in the Ten Commandments and the Sermon on the Mount, that it was corrupt, inefficient, and guilty of oppression and intolerance. With irony and satire as his weapons Voltaire exercised his great influence through scientific treatises, histories, dramas, poems, pamphlets, and even a *Philosophical Dictionary*— not through any one work, but rather through the vast mass of his writings over a long period of time.

Contemporary with Voltaire, and approaching him in universality of influence, was Charles de Secondat, Baron de Montesquieu (1689–1755). Montesquieu early took leave of his judicial calling and devoted the remainder of his life to formulating a theory and technique of politics for mankind in general and for his own countrymen in particular. . . . The great and enduring contribution from Montesquieu's pen . . . was *On the Spirit of Laws*, published in 1748, and providing a learned analysis of political theory and practice, with suggestions as to the possibilities of reform in eighteenth-century France. Taking as his major premise the naturalistic hypothesis of environmental influences, Montesquieu examined the political structures of the past, and classified and explained them according to external conditioning factors. France, he concluded, was designed to be a monarchy, but a monarchy shorn of existing abuses, and with a clearer definition of the powers of the several elements of the government. These elements he defined (on the basis of a mistaken analysis of the British government) as executive, legislative, and judicial, each functioning separately from, and serving as a check on, the others. Where Voltaire was inclined to advocate the destruction of institutions in order to extirpate inherent defects, Montesquieu was disposed to eliminate abuses and, by so doing, to strengthen and preserve the essentials of the institutional forms.

While Voltaire was pointing out the ecclesiastical evils in eighteenth-century France and Montesquieu was suggesting means of reforming the political ills, others were indicating and advocating remedies for the economic inconsistencies of the time. These economists, as they were called, were among the founders of modern political economy, and their contribution to economic theory and practice was extensive and important. For the most part the economists were landowning nobility. They were primarily concerned, therefore, with land as the chief source of wealth. They based their philosophy on the assumption that natural laws govern the economic relationships of men, from which fact they ultimately came to be known as "physiocrats." . . . Outstanding among the exponents of the new economic philosophy were François Quesnay (the King's physician), the Sieur de Gournay, and Pierre Samuel Dupont de Nemours. Although originally concerned only with land, it was inevitable that their ideas should spread to commerce and industry where they served to rationalize the interests of the middle class.

## The Influence of Rousseau

At one with the other thinkers of the time in the attempt to help mankind, yet apart from them in his approach to the problem, was Jean Jacques Rousseau (1712–1778). Born in Geneva of poor parents, and haphazardly self-educated, Rousseau manifested his first serious indication of an interest in humanity in an essay which won the prize in a competition sponsored by the Academy of Dijon in 1749. The essay averred that science and the arts had exercised a retarding influence on human development; and for the remainder of his life Rousseau endeavored to devise remedies for this alleged malady of society. His most influential writings were *Émile*, a treatise on education (1762), and (in the same year) the *Social Contract*, a curious combination of fact and fancy, affording a critique of political, social, and economic organization. Rousseau's assumption in the *Social Contract* was that all men originally were equal and good, but that, owing to their environment, they had become unequal and bad. To be saved from themselves men must return to the happy "state of nature" whence they came, a state which could not be attained until the idea of the social compact was enforced, with the law expressing the general will. Nor could this be done by reason alone as the *philosophes* suggested; even more essential were the "promptings of the heart." It was his emphasis on sentiment which distinguished Rousseau from the *philosophes* and the economists, and which, through the emotional fervor of his writings, gained him a wide reading public despite the derision of his fellow publicists. . . . His service in giving impetus to the doctrine of popular sovereignty ranks him as a vital force in the French Revolution from its very outset.

## How New Ideas Spread

The efforts of the critical publicists of the eighteenth century would have been of slight significance had they not enjoyed a wide audience. The nucleus of such an audience, as already noted, was provided by the ambitious middle class, which sought an ideology to justify its claims to power and prestige; and this nucleus was augmented by liberal intellectuals from the privileged classes. Of great importance to the student of the French Revolution are the means by which the propaganda of the Enlightenment reached this nucleus and spread beyond it. There were many media through which ideas could and did circulate in eighteenth-century France. Coffee shops (cafés), an innovation of the early part of the century, provided meeting places where people might discuss current trends, where news could be disseminated, where even the illiterate could learn what was taking place. Masonic lodges likewise afforded an excellent milieu for the exchange of ideas and opinions. Most important, perhaps, were the salons, where patrons of learning held open house for intellectuals from all walks of life, where old books were analyzed and new ones planned, where existing institutions were examined and changes advocated. Salons became so fashionable, indeed, that many relatively unlettered members of the aristocracy held them because it was the mode.

Pamphlets were perhaps the most universal vehicle for the diffusion of the ideas of the Enlightenment. Until the Revolution, newspapers were few and books were expensive. Pamphlets, however, could be written and printed rapidly, circulated inexpensively, and passed easily from reader to reader. Furthermore, they were a facile means of evading the censorship which, though it declined in severity of application under Louis XVI, still laid burdens on publishers and

## Did the Philosophers Make Rulers More Enlightened?

*As Donald Kagan here explains, the reforms instituted by several European rulers in the mid-1700s were more the result of their personal ambitions than of the enlightening influence of the* philosophes.

Most of the *philosophes* favored neither Montesquieu's reformed and revived aristocracy nor Rousseau's democracy as a solution to contemporary political problems. Like other thoughtful people of the day in other stations and occupations, they looked to the existing monarchies. The *philosophes* hoped in particular that the French monarchy might assert really effective power over the aristocracy and the church to bring about significant reform. Voltaire was a very strong monarchist. He and others— such as Diderot, who visited Catherine II of Russia, and physiocrats who were ministers to the French kings—did not wish to limit the power of monarchs but sought to redirect that power toward the rationalization of economic and political structures and the liberation of intellectual life. Most *philosophes* were not opposed to power if they could find a way of using it for their own purposes.

During the last third of the century it seemed to some observers that several European rulers had actually embraced many of the reforms set forth by the *philosophes. Enlightened absolutism* is the term used to describe this phenomenon. The authors alike. True, relatively few Frenchmen of the Old Regime could read, but many of those who could do so passed their knowledge to their less fortunate fellows by word of mouth. Public opinion, already a force in France, was to achieve greater import under the stimulus of the new propaganda.

One of the most interesting and important propagandist devices of the age was the *Encyclopaedia*, largely the work of Denis Diderot (1713–1784). Diderot's chief object was the organization and systematization of the new ideas, and in collaboration with other intellectuals he produced in the *Encyclopaedia* an elaborate synthesis of the new learning.

phrase indicates monarchical government dedicated to the rational strengthening of the central absolutist administration at the cost of other lesser centers of political power. However, the monarchs most closely associated with it—Frederick II of Prussia, Joseph II of Austria, and Catherine II of Russia—were neither genuinely enlightened nor truly absolute in the exercise of royal power. Their enlightenment was a veneer, and the realities of political and economic life limited their absolutism. . . .

The requirements of state security and political ambition rather than the humanitarian and liberating zeal of the Enlightenment directed the policies of these monarchs. They sought the rational economic and social integration of their realms so that they could wage more efficient future wars—a policy profoundly hateful to the *philosophes*. All of the states of Europe had emerged from the Seven Years' War understanding that they would require stronger armed forces for the next conflict and looking for new sources of taxation to finance those armies. The search for new revenues and further internal political support for their rule led these eastern European monarchs to make "enlightened" reforms. They and their advisers used rationality to further what the *philosophes* considered irrational militarism.

Donald Kagan et al., *The Western Heritage, 1300–1815*. New York: Macmillan, 1983, pp. 635–36.

Everyone of importance in the realm of thought contributed articles to the project. Those who could afford to subscribe to it in advance or to buy it were frequently the ones who would advocate and support most enthusiastically the ideas and information it contained. It is to Diderot, perhaps more than to any other single individual, that the thinkers of the eighteenth century owe the consolidation and propagation of their principles in a form at once dignified and effective.

To thinking Frenchmen of the eighteenth century—and especially to Frenchmen of the middle class—the Enlightenment brought a philosophy of optimism, a theory of progress. By focusing attention on the need for change and by providing the molds in which such change might be cast, its principal exponents facilitated the advent of the Revolution. By the close of the third quarter of the century, France was ripe for such a revolution; and the crisis which was to precipitate it was to come before the end of the reign of the ill-fated Louis XVI.

# Chapter 2

# Significant Events in the Revolutionary Process

# The Estates General and National Assembly

Leo Gershoy

Former New York University scholar Leo Gershoy relates how, to the king's surprise and consternation, the Estates General, which he had expected more or less to maintain the status quo, instead produced the upstart National Assembly, thereby setting the Revolution in motion. As Gershoy points out, the commoners attending the meeting strongly desired meaningful change; and when they were disappointed by the conservative leanings of Jacques Necker, the king's minister of finance, they embraced more progressive leaders, including the powerful orator Honoré Gabriel Mirabeau.

Everywhere except in Paris the elections [to choose delegates to the Estates General] were over in April; and by May 1, 1789, almost all deputies were at Versailles. There were approximately seventeen hundred of them, including the alternates for all the orders. In a variety of petty ways the deputies of the Third Estate were made to feel their inferiority. Their somber and outlandish costumes of black cloth contrasted dismally with the splendid attire worn by the clergy and the nobles. At the formal and highly stilted reception for all the deputies (May 2), the king kept the commoners waiting for hours and then, while the high officials of the court stared at them with condescending curiosity, received them coldly. The formal mass in state which opened the Estates General on May 4 furnished another occasion for humiliation, but the commoners took what comfort they could from the enthusiastic cheers of the townspeople of

Reprinted by permission of Prentice-Hall, Inc., Upper Saddle River, N.J., from *The French Revolution and Napoleon*, by Leo Gershoy, ©Meredith Publishing Company, 1964.

Versailles. After a long, almost interminable, day they retired to await the real opening of the Estates General on the morrow. Their hopes were still fervent, though their spirits had been depressed by the chill of the royal reception.

## Attempts to Maintain the Status Quo

Their disappointment in the king was not abated by what occurred on May 5, but changed from irritation to suspicion. To begin, the royal family delayed proceedings for hours; then the king appeared supposedly to announce the royal program. He read a short speech which was received well enough, though it could scarcely have had less content. The keeper of the royal seals followed with a longer address, which intimated that the crown did not object to the vote by head on financial matters, but opposed such a procedure for the discussion of political reform. Jacques Necker, on whom the commoners pinned their hopes, spoke last and at great length, leaving a spokesman to conclude his address. The king seemed impressed, probably less by the speech than by the applause of the commoners, which implied strongly that it might be unwise to dismiss powerful ministers, as the court faction desired. Necker spoke almost entirely about financial administration and the deficit, explaining that a few reforms and a program of economy would restore financial stability. He avoided the question of constitutional reforms and made hedging allusions to the question of the vote, intimating, however, that on certain matters it would be desirable to vote by order. When Necker's mouthpiece had finished, the master of ceremonies requested all the deputies to show their credentials.

The commoners, as their many commentaries reveal, were aghast at the proceedings. They had come to the capital to serve as true legislators of the nation; now the king and his principal minister served warning that the old order would be maintained, that no opportunity would be given them to "create" a constitution for France, to regenerate the administration and society. Spontaneously, they resolved to resist the policy of the court. They showed their independence by refusing to present their credentials, and the verification was accordingly postponed until the following day. . . .

The events of that day disclosed attitudes and tempers that boded ill for the future. Necker revealed his basic unimaginative mediocrity by failing to grasp the significance of the occasion. He had it in his power to guide the movement for reform under the aegis of the king. But his eye was dimmed to the future; it had grown weary contemplating the figures of receipts and expenditures. He had the soul of a bank clerk; the flame of the statesman did not burn in him. Had Louis XVI been as firm in character as he was benevolent in intention, he might have risen to the heights demanded of a leader. He was not craven, but he was readily influenced by those about him, too open to suggestions; and the suggestions emanating from his court counselors advised him to maintain the *status quo*, to keep the commoners in their place. The commoners were nettled, and in their impatience with the leaders on whom they had counted, but who had failed them, they sought new leaders in their own ranks. Unlike the privileged orders, they refused to verify their credentials separately.

One leader they found in Honoré Gabriel Mirabeau. . . . Experienced, of supple intellect, sure in his political faith of a constitutional monarchy, daring in his acts, and brilliant in oratory, Mirabeau rose rapidly to the leadership of the commoners. When the deputies of the Third Estate, or the Commons as they preferred to call themselves, resolved not to organize a separate body, nor to recognize the verification of the credentials of the deputies save in a common assembly, they adopted a policy that required political finesse and courage. These qualities they found in Mirabeau. With the sure sense of a political realist he directed the united commoners against the weaker of the privileged orders. "Send delegates to the clergy, gentlemen," he cried. "Do not send any to the nobles, for the nobles give orders and the clergy will negotiate."

## Popular Sovereignty Asserted

After five weeks of unseemly bickering over the crucial matter of the organization of the Estates General the commoners ended their inactivity. Upon the initiative of Abbé Sieyès, who had only recently taken his seat with them, and in defiance of the king's express command for the separate verification of credentials, they began to verify not as deputies of the Third Estate, but as representatives of the nation (June 12). During the next few days some of the parish priests came over, and on June 17 the commoners and their adherents among the ecclesiastics, declared themselves the National Assembly of France and proceeded to act as the representative body of the nation.

Their declaration was the first act of the Revolution; indeed, their declaration contained the whole theory and achievement of the Revolution. In a few deliberate and coldly logical phrases they set aside the entire theory and practice of a government and society based upon privileged orders and asserted the democratic theory of numbers and of popular sovereignty. "The denomination of National Assembly is the only one which is suitable for the Assembly in the present condition of things; because the members who compose it are the only representatives lawfully and publicly known and verified; because they are sent directly by almost the totality of the nation; because, lastly, the representation being one and indivisible, none of the deputies in whatever class or order he may be chosen, has the right to exercise his functions apart from the present Assembly." The commoners represented "at least ninety-six per cent of the nation"; therefore they constituted the National Assembly. The Assembly took pains to reassure the creditors of the state that the debt would be paid, ordered the provisional collection of the existing taxes, declared that new taxes were not valid without its consent, and denied the king the right to veto its future resolutions. Two days later, June 19, Mirabeau's expectations were realized, for by a small majority the clergy voted to join the Commons in the National Assembly and in that way gave indorsement to the illegal and revolutionary act of June 17.

At once the court party, led by the queen and the count of Artois, the younger of the two brothers of Louis XVI, urged the harried monarch to take repressive measures; while Necker, equally insistent, outlined a program of reforms.

Louis XVI half acquiesced in Necker's view, but at the same
time he had decided to annul the measures of the Commons.
Despite Necker's objections he made plans to hold a "royal
session" of the Estates General on June 22, on which occasion he intended to announce the policy of the court on the
manner of voting and the question of reforms and thus settle the constitutional dispute which had made impossible the
solution of the nation's problems. . . .

## The King Forced to Yield

The immediate future of France lay with Louis XVI. He
could have summoned the troops against the rebellious deputies, but such a course would have been catastrophic to
France. He determined to intimidate the commoners with
*threats* of force. He rejected Necker's conciliatory plan and
postponed the royal session to June 23. Meantime a majority of the clergy and a bare sprinkling of noblemen joined
the deputies of the Third Estate in the hall of the National
Assembly. The Assembly was now composed of the majority
of orders as well as of deputies.

Louis XVI was ready with his program on June 23. Before
the royal session opened the commoners received a taste of
what was to come. In spite of a heavy rain they were kept
waiting for an hour before they were admitted. . . . Spectators
were excluded and a detachment of troops surrounded the
hall. Necker's seat was empty, which gave rise to the rumor
that he had resigned, though in fact his resignation in protest
over the king's policy did not come until after the session.

The speech delivered by the king gave point to the obvious preparations that had been made to intimidate the
deputies of the Third Estate. He spoke coldly, with majestic
haughtiness ignoring the resolutions of June 17 and June 20.
It was his royal wish to have "the ancient distinction of the
three orders of the state maintained in its entirety." Subject
to his approval, certain stipulated matters might be discussed
in common, but constitutional questions were to be discussed separately. Having stated his policy on the disputed
points, the monarch outlined the royal program of reform
and indicated how far he was ready to go. All property rights

without exception (signifying ecclesiastical and feudal property) were to be respected; and no change was to be made in the organization of the army. On the other hand the king promised wide and important financial powers to the Estates General, agreed to the abolition of the most obnoxious feudal and fiscal abuses, and promised equality of taxation to his subjects. He signified his readiness to grant the basic rights of personal liberty to all citizens and ordered the establishment of provincial estates throughout the realm.

Submitted to the Estates General on May 5, the king's program would undoubtedly have served as a basis for discussion. On June 23 it was outmoded since the Commons not only had gone beyond the royal program, but had taken a solemn oath to do that which the king forbade; namely, to draw up a new constitution. Consequently, his final words, an unveiled threat to dismiss the Estates General and carry out his plans alone, if the commoners would not coöperate with him, and his command for the immediate separation of the three orders thrust the decision squarely upon the deputies of the Third Estate. The nobles and most of the clergy followed Louis XVI as he left the hall, but the commoners defied him and his threats. When the master of ceremonies repeated the royal command . . . the thundering voice of Mirabeau filled the hall: "Go and tell those who sent you that we are here by the will of the people, and that we will go only if we are driven at the point of the bayonet." Sieyès in his cold, imperturbable fashion proposed that the Assembly pass a resolution that it adhered to all its previous declarations. The resolution was passed. On Mirabeau's plea the Assembly voted that whoever attacked the inviolability of a deputy (arrested him for what he said in the Assembly) was guilty of a treasonable act punishable by death. Now the decision lay with Louis XVI, rather than with the commoners. He could choose between crushing the rebels or yielding. For the present he chose to yield and gave an order for the withdrawal of the royal bodyguard that had invested the hall.

# The Fall of the Bastille

Simon Schama

This vivid telling of one of the most famous incidents of the Revolution is taken from historian Simon Schama's *Citizens: A Chronicle of the French Revolution*, a work recently hailed as one of the greatest books ever written on the subject. Schama captures the personal plight of the Bastille's commanding officer, Bernard-René de Launay, a man in the wrong place at the wrong time, as well as the unreasoning fury of the Paris mob, which was driven by suspicions that weapons and gunpowder were stored at the Hôtel des Invalides (or simply the Invalides) and the Bastille, both manned mainly by small garrisons of *invalides*, retired soldiers.

Bernard-René de Launay had been born in the Bastille, where his father had been governor, and he would die on the evening of the fourteenth of July in the shadow of its towers. . . .

On the fourteenth of July he was, with good reason, apprehensive. . . . The commandant of the Invalides had sent him the huge consignment of 250 barrels of powder (about thirty thousand pounds), yet he had only a modest force with which to defend it. In response to an urgent request for reinforcements, he had been given, on July 7, a further thirty-two men from the Swiss Salis-Samade regiment to add to the eighty-two *invalides* pensioners stationed there. . . . The *invalides* were unlikely to defend the fortress to the last man. Worst of all, in the event of siege, the Bastille had only a two-day supply of food and no internal supply of water at all. In the end, that was what probably decided its capitulation [surrender].

In front of the outer courtyard were gathered about nine hundred Parisians. They included a few men of standing and property. . . . There were also a sizable number of defecting soldiers and *gardes françaises* [members of the king's royal guard]. But making up by far the largest number were local artisans living in the faubourg Saint-Antoine—joiners, cabinetmakers, hatters, locksmiths, cobblers, tailors and the like. There were also a good number—twenty-one according to the official list of the *vainqueurs de la Bastille* [those citizens who participated in the Bastille's fall]—of wine merchants, which is to say owners of the *cabarets* that served as well as sold wine and which were the headquarters of neighborhood gossip and politics. One of them, Claude Cholat, whose wine shop was in the rue Noyer, produced a justly famous "primitive" graphic rendering of the day's events. Of the six hundred of whom we have information, as many as four hundred in the crowd had immigrated to Paris from the provinces, and since July 14 saw the price of the four-pound loaf reach a record high, most of their families were undoubtedly hungry.

They were also prey to considerable fear. During the night rumors had circulated that troops were about to march or were already on their way from Sèvres and Saint-Denis to crush the Paris rising. And the Bastille seemed to be heavily munitioned, with fifteen eight-pounder cannon on the towers and a further three in the inner courtyard pointing at the gates. Twelve more guns on the ramparts could fire pound-and-a-half balls, and in his nervousness de Launay had even assembled a bizarre collection of siege missiles like paving stones and rusty ironmongery to drop on the assailants, should that be necessary.

## Initial Negotiations

The initial aim of the crowd was simply to neutralize the guns and to take possession of the powder. To this end, two delegates from the Hôtel de Ville asked to see the governor, and since it was around ten in the morning they were invited in for *déjeuner* [breakfast or early lunch]. Even by the standards of the last day of the *ancien régime*, this seemed a lengthy entertainment. The crowd, from the beginning, had been suspicious when de Launay had refused entry to any but the two delegates and had demanded three "hostage" soldiers in exchange. The prolonged lunch . . . deepened those suspicions. A second deputy, Thuriot de La Rozière, was sent for from the district headquarters of Saint-Louis-la-Culture, and he too was admitted to see de Launay, this time armed with specific instructions. The guns, along with their powder, should be removed and delivered to the militia representing the city of Paris, and a unit of the militia should be admitted to the Bastille. This, de Launay replied, was impossible until he had received instructions from Versailles, but he took Thuriot up to the ramparts to inspect the withdrawal of the guns.

It was about half past twelve. Not much had been achieved on either side. None of the essential demands made by Thuriot had been granted, and although he had made efforts to persuade the *invalides* to come to some agreement with the people, de Launay's officers had insisted that it would be dishonorable to hand over the fortress without express orders from their seniors. Thuriot decided to report back to the electors at the Hôtel de Ville for further negotiating instructions. They were themselves reluctant to inflame the situation, and at half past one Thuriot was about to return to the Bastille with another elector, Ethis de Corny, equipped with bugle and loud-hailer by which the removal of the guns would be announced to the people, when the Hôtel de Ville shook to the sound of an explosion followed by the crackle of musket fire coming from the fort.

## The Battle Begins

While he had been gone, the impatience of the crowd had finally burst its bounds. Shouts of "Give us the Bastille" were heard, and the nine hundred had pressed into the undefended outer courtyard, becoming angrier by the minute. A group, including an ex-soldier now carriage maker, had climbed onto the roof of a perfume shop abutting the gate to the inner courtyard and, failing to find the keys to the courtyard, had cut the drawbridge chains. They had crashed down without warning, killing one of the crowd who stood beneath, and over the bridge and his body poured hundreds of the besiegers. At this point the defending soldiers shouted to the people to withdraw or else they would fire, and this too was misinterpreted as encouragement to come further. The first shots were fired. Subsequently each side would claim the other fired first, but since no one among the melee knew that their own people had cut the drawbridge, it was assumed that they had been let into the inner courtyard in order to be mowed down in the confined space by the cannon. . . .

The battle became serious. At about half past three in the afternoon the crowd was reinforced by companies of *gardes françaises* and by defecting soldiers, including a number who were veterans of the American campaign. Two in particular, Second-Lieutenant Jacob Elie, the standard-bearer of the Infantry of the Queen, and Pierre-Augustin Hulin, the director of the Queen's laundry, were crucial in turning the incoherent assault into an organized siege. . . .

Hulin and Elie also brought an ample supply of arms taken from the Invalides that morning. With them were two cannon, one bronze and the other the Siamese gun inlaid with silver that had been seized from the royal storehouse the day before. . . .

A wooden gate now divided the cannon of the besiegers from those of the defenders—perhaps a hundred feet apart. Had they opened up at each other, dreadful carnage would have been guaranteed. But if the attackers could not see the defending guns, the defending troops were well aware of the peril they stood in. Faced with the increasing reluctance of the *invalides* to prolong the fighting, de Launay was himself demoralized. In any case, there was no food with which to withstand a prolonged siege, so that his main concern now was for a surrender that would preserve the honor and the lives of the garrison. He had one card—the powder. In his darkest moments he simply thought of exploding the entire store—and destroying a large part of the faubourg Saint-Antoine—rather than capitulating. Dissuaded from this act of desperation, he resolved to use the threat at least to secure an honorable evacuation.

## The Surrender

With no white flag available, a handkerchief was flown from one of the towers and the Bastille's guns stopped firing. At around five, a note asking for such a capitulation, written by the governor—and threatening the explosion unless it was given—was stuck through a chink in the drawbridge wall of the inner courtyard. A plank was laid down over the moat with men standing on one end to steady it. The first person on the plank fell into the moat but the second—whose identity thereafter was hotly disputed—retrieved it. The demand, however, was refused, and in response to the continued anger of the crowd Hulin was apparently preparing to fire the Siamese cannon when the drawbridge suddenly came down.

The *vainqueurs* rushed into the prison, liberated all seven of the prisoners, took possession of the gunpowder and disarmed the defending troops. The Swiss guards, who had prudently taken off their uniform coats, were initially mistaken for prisoners and unharmed. But some of the *invalides* were brutally dealt with. A soldier named Béquard, who had been one of those responsible for dissuading de Launay from detonating the gunpowder, had his hand severed almost as soon as he opened one of the gates of the fort. Under the impression that he was one of the prison warders, the crowd paraded the hand about the streets still gripping a key. Later that evening he was misidentified again, this time as one of the cannoneers who had first fired on the people, and was hanged in the place de Grève, along with one of his comrades, before the thirty Swiss guards lined up as an obligatory audience.

The battle itself had taken the lives of eighty-three of the citizens' army. Another fifteen were to die from wounds. Only one of the *invalides* had died in the fighting and three had been wounded. The imbalance was enough for the crowd to demand some sort of punitive sacrifice, and de Launay duly provided it. All of the hatred which to a large degree had been spared the garrison was concentrated on him. His attributes of command—a sword and baton—were wrenched away from him and he was marched towards the Hôtel de

Ville through enormous crowds, all of whom were convinced he had been foiled in a diabolical plot to massacre the people. Hulin and Elie managed to prevent the crowd from killing him on the street, though more than once he was knocked down and badly beaten. Throughout the walk he was covered in abuse and spittle. Outside the Hôtel de Ville competing suggestions were offered as to how he should meet his end, including a proposal to tie him to a horse's tail and drag him over the cobbles. A pastry cook named Desnot said it would be better to take him into the Hôtel de Ville—but at that point de Launay, who had had enough of the ordeal, shouted "Let me die" and lashed out with his boots, landing a direct hit in Desnot's groin. He was instantaneously covered with darting knives, swords and bayonets, rolled to the gutter and finished off with a barrage of pistol shots. . . .

A sword was handed to Desnot, but he cast it aside and used a pocketknife to saw through de Launay's neck. A little later, de Flesselles . . . who had also been accused of deliberately misleading the people about stores of arms, was shot as he emerged, from the Hôtel de Ville. The heads were stuck on pikes that bobbed and dipped above cheering, laughing and singing crowds that filled the streets. . . .

More than the actual casualties of fighting (which, as we have seen, were very limited), it was this display of punitive sacrifice that constituted a kind of revolutionary sacrament. Some, who had celebrated the Revolution so long as it was expressed in abstractions like *Liberté*, gagged at the sight of blood thrust in their faces. Others whose nerves were tougher and stomachs less easily turned made the modern compact by which power could be secured through violence. The beneficiaries of this bargain deluded themselves into believing that they could turn it on and off like a faucet and direct its force with exacting selectivity. Barnave, the Grenoble politician who in 1789 was among the unreserved zealots of the National Assembly, was asked whether the deaths . . . were really necessary to secure freedom. He gave the reply which, converted into an instrument of the revolutionary state, would be the entitlement to kill him on the guillotine: "What, then, is their blood so pure?"

# The Great Fear and the Night of August 4

Gaetano Salvemini

As Italian scholar Gaetano Salvemini, former professor of history at the University of Florence, here explains, the abolition of feudal rights and obligations in the Assembly's famous and dramatic session of August 4, 1789, was not, at least on paper, as sweeping a series of reforms as is often supposed. At the time, most of the Assembly's members were property owners and, not surprisingly, they wanted to protect their own properties and privileges. However, Salvemini points out, because the peasants simply ignored the Assembly's new rules, the old feudal aspects of the French system did effectively end on August 4.

After July 14th [1789, the date of the fall of the Bastille prison to a Paris mob], the King of France was king in name only. In Paris, the mob, having once tasted freedom from restraint, was not easily to be subjected again to the rule of law. On July 22nd, the seventy-four-year-old Intendant of Finance Foulon and his son-in-law Bertier, Intendant of Paris, both of them contractors for the commissariat of the army concentrated near the capital before July 14th, were seized and brutally murdered. In other cities, the former state officials were by now reduced to impotence; many had fled, or gone into hiding, if they had not joined the ranks of the insurgents. Customs-barriers were pulled down, grain-stores plundered, and the taxes left uncollected. All those suspected of opposition to the *tiers état* [third estate] went in danger of death.

From *The French Revolution, 1788–1792*, by Gaetano Salvemini, translated by I.M. Rawson. (London: Jonathan Cape, 1954). Reprinted by permission of Random House UK.

Even graver and more widespread was the convulsion in the countryside. To the peasants, who cared nothing for politics but were anxiously awaiting an end to taxation and feudal dues, the Paris revolution and the lesser revolutions which broke out in provincial cities were sparks setting off a train of powder that had been prepared long since. At first, a sense of confused terror filled their hearts: the *grande peur* [great fear], which left an indelible impression on the people's minds. They deserted their villages, took refuge in caves and forests, gathered into bands and armed themselves against a danger which, in their over-heated imaginations, was the more fearful for being undefined. Once their panic had subsided they found themselves united and in arms. Then they turned upon those evils that were familiar and near at hand. There were to be no more taxes, no more feudal dues: the King and the Assembly had decided; the law had been passed and must be carried out. In eastern and central France, especially, the peasants were not content with merely passive repudiation. They imitated, in their own way, the taking of the Bastille, and attacked *châteaux* [country mansions] and monasteries, burning manorial rolls and the records of their feudal obligations, and leaving the buildings a heap of ruins. If the noble or prelate resisted or was suspected of opposing them they forced him to sign away all the rights of which he stood possessed, and then, in many cases, murdered him with his family or household.

## The Assembly Alarmed

The majority in the National Assembly—commons, liberal nobility and lower clergy—were themselves surprised at so vast a landslide of events. Suspecting the Court of plotting behind their backs they at first welcomed the revolt of the populace, which seemed not inopportune, since it at least had the advantage of disarming the Government. The Assembly, therefore, confined itself for some days to passing harmless resolutions exhorting the citizens to restore order and to show themselves worthy of the freedom they had won. As time went on, however, news from the provinces grew increasingly grave, and the Assembly became alarmed.

ғroperty of all kinds,' declared a deputy at the sitting of August 3rd, 'is a prey to brigandage; everywhere the *châteaux* are being burnt, monasteries destroyed and farms plundered. Taxes and feudal dues remain unpaid, the laws are not enforced, the magistrates are powerless and justice is unobtainable in the courts.' He went on to propose that a statement should be issued condemning the disorders as 'contrary to the principles of common law, which the Assembly will never cease to uphold'.

At the afternoon session of August 4th, one of the Paris deputies, the lawyer Target, suggested the issue of another proclamation declaring payment of taxes and respect for feu-

## The Assembly's Decree on Feudalism

*These are some of the articles of the famous decree issued by the National Assembly on August 4 and finalized on August 11. Although the members of the Assembly attempted only to modify the old feudal order, the peasants interpreted the opening sentence of article 1 in a more literal and radical manner.*

Article 1. The National Assembly overthrows the feudal regime entirely. It decrees that those rights and dues, whether feudal or rental, which derive from real or personal mortmain and from personal servitude, . . . are abolished without indemnity. All others are declared redeemable, and the price and manner of redemption shall be determined by the National Assembly. Those aforesaid dues which are not suppressed by this decree, however, shall continue to be levied until reimbursement is completed. . . .

3. The exclusive right of hunting and open warrens is likewise abolished, and every landowner has the right to destroy or have destroyed, but only on his own holdings, every kind of game, provided he conforms to police regulations which may be made relative to public security. . . .

4. All seigneurial courts of law [those held by nobles over their peasants] are suppressed without any indemnity; nevertheless, the officers of those courts shall continue their duties until the National Assembly has provided for the establishment of a new judicial order. . . .

dal rights obligatory until such time as the law decided otherwise. But proclamations could avail little, so long as the Assembly had no effective means of imposing its will. This was fully realized by the nobles, who had most to gain from a return to normal conditions. The Vicomte de Noailles explained that it was necessary to suppress the cause of the rioting and thus cure the evil at its roots; he therefore proposed that the Assembly should proclaim proportional taxation, an end of feudal dues, the opening of civil and military posts to citizens of every class, abolition, without indemnity, of the corvées [forced labor of peasants, especially on road repair] and remains of serfdom, and free redemption

8. Casual fees due to country priests are suppressed and shall cease to be paid as soon as provision has been made for augmenting their emoluments [privileges that come with their position] and for paying vicars. A regulation shall be made to determine the lot of city priests.

9. Pecuniary [monetary] privileges, personal or real, relating to taxation, are abolished forever. The levy shall be raised from all citizens, and on all possessions, in the same manner and the same form. Means shall be considered to bring about proportional payment of contributions, even for the last six months of the current financial year.

10. Because a national constitution and public liberty are of greater advantage to the provinces than the privileges which some enjoy, the sacrifice of which is essential for the close union of all parts of the Empire, all special privileges of provinces, principalities, localities, cantons, cities and communities of inhabitants, whether pecuniary, or of any other nature, are declared abolished permanently and shall be merged into the law common to all Frenchmen.

11. All citizens, without distinction of birth, may be admitted to every employment and every ecclesiastical, civil or military dignity, and no useful profession shall entail loss of rank.

D.I. Wright, ed., *The French Revolution: Introductory Documents*. St. Lucia: University of Queensland Press, 1974, pp. 52–54.

of all other feudal rights. The Duc d'Aiguillon, too, one of the richest feudal lords of France, admitted that feudal charges and unjust taxation were a cause of the disturbances; but, he observed, if equality of taxation were to be introduced immediately, it would be wrong to abolish feudal dues without indemnity, since they too were a form of private property. He therefore proposed that they should continue to be paid, unless commuted by a capital payment corresponding to the annual value of each charge, multiplied by thirty. The same idea regarding commutation was put forward by a Breton deputy, Leguen de Kérangall, who wished to have the 'infamous title-deeds' preserving these unjust rights, 'acquired in dark and ignorant times', consigned to the purifying flames.

Surrounded in the great hall by an excited public and influenced not only by the philosophy and humanitarianism of the time but by genuine alarm at the course events were taking, the whole body of deputies became imbued, little by little, with a frenzy of enthusiasm. The Marquis de Foucault condemned the privileges of the court nobility. The Vicomte de Beauharnais demanded that all citizens should be eligible for public office. The Bishop of Nancy proposed redemption of the Church's feudal rights. The Bishop of Chartres wanted to abolish all privileges of the chase. The Duc du Châtelet proposed redemption of ecclesiastical tithes. The Assembly agreed and applauded. Thus one by one the privileges of the seigniorial hunt, the seigniorial pigeon-cote, and those of the feudal courts and trade-guilds were all done away with. Serfdom was abolished. Representatives from the provincial cities and country districts renounced their local municipal and fiscal privileges. Finally, the Assembly ordered a medal to be struck commemorating the great occasion, and endowed Louis XVI with the title of 'Restorer of French Liberty'. At eight in the morning, when the session adjourned amid acclamation and the deputies separated after embracing one another, the old feudal society of France had legally disappeared. . . .

The whole body of deputies had, in fact, been carried away by genuine enthusiasm, and even those who were, in truth, only sacrificing the rights of others, sincerely felt that they were doing great things for their country. It is, however, undeniable that had the nobles and clergy surrendered their privileges a month earlier, their merit would have been morally greater, and they might well have prevented or at least lessened the gravity of the crisis. As it was, they only gave legal recognition to destruction that had, in many places, already taken place.

## Some Feudal Charges Retained

Nor must it be forgotten that while certain relics of feudalism, such as immunity from taxation, the *corvée*, serfdom, and monopolistic and judicial privileges, were abolished without indemnity [compensation]—which was the really generous aspect of these decisions—other feudal charges were declared computable by capitalizing the revenue at about 3⅓ per cent. The rural population could not possibly raise the enormous sums required for carrying out such an operation. . . . It is obvious, therefore, that on August 4th the Assembly, in abolishing a part of the feudal rights, was hoping to safeguard the more important by forcing the peasants to redeem them [pay a fee in exchange for their elimination].

Furthermore, so soon as it became necessary to embody these resolutions in legal form, every member of the privileged classes hastened to rescue what property he could from the wreck. The deputies of the *tiers état*, nearly all of whom were townsmen indifferent to the peasants' claims or else opposed to them because themselves possessed of feudal rights, put up no resistance to these maneuvers.

Feudal rights were classified as either personal or real; the former were abolished without indemnity, and the latter declared redeemable. Owing to the difficulty of making a clear distinction between them the Assembly instituted an extremely complicated schedule of individual cases, in the course of which very few rights were abolished altogether, and nearly all became redeemable. Redemption was hedged about with a thousand restrictions and formalities. All existing rights were assumed to be legitimate. In cases where this was contested the obligation to prove illegality was placed upon the peasants; and since proof was almost impossible to provide, the outcome of such disputes was a foregone conclusion. The original intention having thus been side-tracked, the provisions were embodied in the decrees of August 4th–11th, and subsequently developed and brought to completion in those of March 15th–28th, 1790: the first article of which opened with the words: 'The National Assembly has put an end to the feudal régime'; while the succeeding ones, by citing innumerable exceptions, re-established, to a considerable extent, the former order of things.

On one point only was the Assembly more generous than it had been on the night of August 4th: that of ecclesiastical tithes. The latter, which at first had been declared redeemable, were abolished without compensation for the Church, except that the Government undertook in future to maintain the clergy. The land was thus relieved of an annual burden of 120 millions. But these millions were for the most part swallowed up by the big landowners—the nobles thus reimbursing themselves for loss of their feudal rights at the clergy's expense—while the farmers and peasantry gained little. On the other hand, the expense of maintaining the clergy, having been taken over by the nation, now fell on the taxpayers, whether they owned land or not.

This first attempt at legislation by the Assembly, therefore, was characteristic of all its later policy, and showed the contrast between its courageous intentions and the often petty meanness of its actions. The deputies, theory-ridden as they were and politically inexperienced, turned every question into one of principle: an absolute principle of equity and justice, or rather of what, in eighteenth-century opinion, stood for equity and justice. But so soon as concrete consequences had to be drawn from abstract principles, individual interests, habits and passions became involved, and led to the making of innumerable exceptions to what were intended as universally beneficent reforms. In this way, many contradictory and mutilated laws, of advantage only to the property-owning classes who formed a majority in the Assembly, were passed. It was a strange mixture of enthusiasm and prudence, of ingenuousness and cunning, that perplexes the historian and makes these early representatives of modern France appear, at one moment, quixotic doctrinaires pursuing unattainable ideals, and at the next, shrewd business-men, bent on extorting all possible advantage for themselves from the general ruin.

But the peasants, unable to follow distinctions and exceptions set forth by legal experts, cared nothing for the Assembly's decrees, just as they had not asked its permission before abolishing feudalism on their own account, after the Paris revolution. They accepted the one article declaring the feudal régime entirely suppressed, and refused to obey the rest. While the nobles and clergy, encouraged by the tortuous proceedings in the Assembly, insisted on respect not only for those rights declared legitimate, but also for those that had been abolished, the peasants would recognize none of them. They went hunting and fishing to demonstrate the end of the seigniorial game-laws, continued to attack abbeys and *châteaux*, and passed resolutions at their meetings to the effect that anyone paying feudal dues should be hanged. When National Guards were sent to check their destructive fury, they repulsed them by force of arms. Every law passed by the Assembly with the aim of breaking down their stubborn resistance was without effect: the havoc they wrought, or such restraint as they showed being the outcome, not of the Assembly's decisions but simply of their own needs, desires and passions.

It was not, therefore, one revolution only but two independent revolutions: in the towns the aim of the commons was to deprive the privileged classes of their political power; and in the countryside, to root out every vestige of feudalism and to win personal freedom and full ownership of the land. The two revolutions at times became merged together, but were often in conflict; not seldom each disavowed the other, but in reality they gave one another mutual support. . . . But by taking place together and with converging aims, the two revolutions assailed the privileged orders and the Government from every side, bewildering and overwhelming them with a flood of revolutionary action impossible to stem.

# The Declaration of the Rights of Man and Citizen

## Lynn Hunt

The declaration, adopted by the French National Assembly on August 26, 1789, expresses some of the same sentiments as the 1776 American Declaration of Independence and the 1776 Virginia Bill of Rights (much of which was incorporated in the American Bill of Rights). As University of Pennsylvania scholar Lynn Hunt explains, this was no accident; the deputies of the National Assembly were definitely influenced by the American revolutionaries. Hunt goes on to summarize the debate over the French declaration and its subsequent profound influence on societies worldwide.

The American War of Independence had helped make notions of human rights even more influential in France, for many of the French officers who served in North America arrived home fired by the ideals of liberty that they saw in action in the New World. Thomas Jefferson's Declaration of Independence of 1776 put the Enlightenment position on rights into a declarative, political form: "We hold these truths to be self-evident: that all men are created equal; that they are endowed by their Creator with certain inalienable rights; that among these are life, liberty and the pursuit of happiness"—happiness being an Enlightenment addition to Locke's original list of rights. The protection of these rights justified colonial resistance to Great Britain, but this was as far as the declaration went; it had no legal relationship to the constitutions written later.

## British and American Precedents

When declaring their rights the Americans drew on the constitutional tradition that they had inherited from the English. English Parliaments regularly cited King John's Great Charter of English liberties, the Magna Carta of 1215. The constitutional conflicts between the English Crown and Parliament in the seventeenth century inspired a renewal of the declaratory urge, as Parliament forced Charles I to accept a Petition of Right in 1628 and then insisted that the newly crowned William and Mary agree to a Bill of Rights in 1689. These documents reaffirmed the "ancient rights and liberties" of Englishmen as represented in English common law and the customary relations between Crown and Parliament; they grew out of English legal traditions and constitutional quarrels rather than a universal human rights philosophy. Locke's writings, forged in the midst of these very English struggles, helped turn the idea of rights and liberties in a more universalistic direction.

The idea of proclaiming a bill of rights passed over into the rebellious American colonies in the 1770s, where several state legislatures drew up such bills when they wrote new state constitutions. The most influential of these was the Virginia Bill of Rights, drafted by George Mason and adopted in 1776. It clearly influenced the French deputies when they met in 1789. The first article of the Virginia Bill of Rights held "That all men are by nature equally free and independent, and have certain inherent rights . . . namely, the enjoyment of life and liberty, with the means of acquiring and possessing property, and pursuing and obtaining happiness and safety." Like Jefferson's Declaration of Independence, the Virginia Bill of Rights proclaimed the rights of *all* men, not just Americans or Virginians. The new U.S. Congress began its discussion of a federal bill of rights at about the same time as the deputies in the new French National Assembly considered drafting a declaration of their own. The idea of making a solemn declaration of rights was definitely in the air.

## Debate About Proclaiming Rights

On June 17, 1789, after six weeks of inconclusive debate about voting procedures, the deputies of the Third Estate proclaimed themselves the true representatives of the nation; they invited the deputies from the two other orders to join them as deputies of a National Assembly. By the stroke of a pen—once the deputies of the clergy and the nobility began to join them—the Third Estate had transformed the political situation of the country, and as the National Assembly it turned to writing a constitution based on new principles. Many believed that the constitution must be preceded by a declaration of rights. Marquis de Lafayette, one of the most celebrated French participants in the American War of Independence and a close friend of Thomas Jefferson, offered the first proposal on July 11, 1789.

Events quickly overtook the discussion. On July 13 the people of Paris learned that Louis XVI had secretly fired his finance minister Jacques Necker, a supporter of the Third Es-

## An Author of the Declaration Recalls Its Inception

*Pierre Dumont, a political writer who assisted the popular leader Mirabeau in the early days of the National Assembly, later published his recollections of the debates on and drafting of the rights declaration, which ironically, Dumont claims, he considered an unnecessary document that would soon be forgotten.*

The idea was American, and there was scarcely a member who did not consider such a declaration an indispensable preliminary. I well remember the long debate on the subject, which lasted several weeks, as a period of mortal ennui [weariness and boredom]. There were silly disputes about words, much metaphysical trash, and dreadfully tedious prosing. The Assembly had converted itself into a Sorbonne [university], and each apprentice in the art of legislation was trying his yet unfledged wings upon such puerilities. After the rejection of several models, a committee of five members was appointed to present a new one. Mirabeau, one of the five, undertook the work with his usual generosity, but imposed its execution upon his friends. He set about the task, and there were he, Duroveray, Clavière,

tate. Bands of Parisians began to arm themselves. On July 14 an armed crowd attacked the most imposing symbol of royal power in the city of Paris, the huge Bastille prison. When the garrison capitulated, the crowd cut off the head of the prison governor and paraded it through the streets. Parisians acted because they feared that the movement of thousands of army troops into their city presaged an attack on the new National Assembly, which met nearby in Versailles. The king had to back away from any such plan, if indeed he had one. The old leaders, from the king on down, began to lose their authority. Discussion of a declaration of rights now took place in a much tenser and more uncertain atmosphere, but it seemed, if anything, more urgent than ever.

When debate focused in August on the declaration it revealed a great diversity of opinion about the desirability of

---

and I writing, disputing, adding, striking out, and exhausting both time and patience upon this ridiculous subject. At length we produced our piece of patchwork, our mosaic of pretended natural rights which never existed. . . . *Men are born free and equal!* that is not true. They are not born free; on the contrary, they are born in a state of weakness and necessary dependence. *Equal!* how are they so, or how can they be so? If by equality is understood equality of fortune, of talents, of virtue, of industry, or of rank, then the falsehood is manifest. It would require volumes of argument to give any reasonable meaning to that equality proclaimed without exception. In a word, my opinion against the declaration of the rights of man was so strongly formed that this time it influenced that of our little committee. Mirabeau, on presenting the project, even ventured to make some objections to it, and proposed to defer the declaration of rights until the constitution should be completed. "I can safely predict," said he, in his bold and energetic style, "that any declaration of rights anterior to [coming before] the constitution will prove but the almanac of a single year!"

Quoted in E.L. Higgins, ed., *The French Revolution as Told by Contemporaries.* Boston: Houghton Mifflin, 1939, pp. 110–11.

making any kind of proclamation of specific rights. This division of opinion continued down to the present; did the proclamation of rights provide the only viable basis for the government's legitimacy, or did it only create unreasonable expectations in a society that could not immediately deliver on the promise of equality? The influence of American models made itself felt in the discussion, but the French deputies clearly aimed for something even more universal: As Duke Mathieu de Montmorency exhorted, " [the Americans] have set a great example in the new hemishpere; let us give one to the universe." Even at this very early stage of discussion, the connection between natural rights and democracy as a form of government had already emerged; some argued that democracy might be suitable to the Americans with their custom of equality but could not be introduced in France, with its heritage of feudalism and aristocratic privilege.

Prominent deputies, including Abbé Sieyès and Marquis de Lafayette, rushed their proposed declarations into print for all to consider. In the end, however, the National Assembly adopted as its text for debate a compromise document drawn up collectively by one of its own subcommittees. In the ensuing discussion, the deputies modified and pared down the subcommittee's original twenty-four articles to seventeen. After six days of debate (August 20–24 and August 26), they voted to postpone any further discussion until after drawing up a new constitution. They never reopened the question. Thus the declaration comprised the seventeen articles that could be agreed on during those six days of debate.

## The Declaration's Enduring Influence

However much the subject of political negotiation and compromise at the time, the declaration exercised an enduring influence on all subsequent discussions of human rights. Like the Declaration of Independence and the Virginia Bill of Rights of 1776, the Declaration of the Rights of Man and Citizen spoke the language of "the natural, inalienable and sacred rights of man." But unlike its predecessors, it stood as the preamble to the constitution and provided the principles of political legitimacy. In the United States the Bill of Rights served to protect citizens from government and was composed only after the constitution itself was ratified; in France the declaration of rights provided the basis for government itself and was consequently drafted before the constitution.

The Declaration of the Rights of Man and Citizen laid out a vision of government based on principles completely different from those of the monarchy. According to the declaration, the legitimacy of government must now flow from the guarantee of individual rights by the law. Under the monarchy, legitimacy depended on the king's will and his maintenance of a historic order that granted privileges according to rank and status. Most remarkably, the deputies of 1789 endeavored to make a statement of universal application, rather than one particularly or uniquely French, and it is that universality that has ensured the continuing resonance of the document. In 1793 and again in 1795 new assemblies drew up new declarations, but these never enjoyed the prestige or authority of the 1789 declaration.

# The King's Fall from Power, Trial, and Execution

Norah Lofts and Margery Weiner

In this lively, informative excerpt from their popular history of France, English historians Norah Lofts and Margery Weiner recount Louis XVI's steadily declining fortunes between late 1789 and early 1793, as he suffered humiliation, house arrest, imprisonment, and eventually trial and execution. Radicals like Robespierre thought that eliminating the king would legitimize and facilitate further stages of the Revolution, but in the sober light of history their regicide seems little more than a paranoid, cruel, and unnecessary act.

Louis was, naturally, hesitant to give his blessing to a declaration which destroyed his absolute power; the Paris mob was, naturally, impatient. Rumor, as always, was busy. It was said that although the King had accepted and worn the *tricolore* in Paris, in Versailles it was being trodden underfoot; it was said that the King, encouraged by dissension within the Assembly, refused to ratify its decrees. A busy and well-fed community might have shrugged off such rumors or waited for their confirmation but the people of Paris were still unemployed and still hungry. Much had happened since May when the States-General met; much had happened since July when the people had first shown their claws, but nothing yet had provided jobs, or loaves. . . .

## The Royal Family Forced to Leave Versailles

By October patience was running out; even the season may have influenced men's moods; winter, always hardest on the

From *Eternal France: A History of France from the French Revolution Through World War II*, by Norah Lofts and Margery Weiner. Copyright Norah Lofts and Margery Weiner, 1968. Reproduced with permission of Curtis Brown Ltd., London, on behalf of the Estates of Norah Lofts and Margery Weiner.

poor, was imminent. On the fifth, despite the rain, the crowd set off to trudge the twelve miles to Versailles, "to see the King," they said.

It is fashionable at the moment to stress the middle-class character of the Revolution; men of the middle class, lawyers, journalists, together with members of the aristocracy such as Mirabeau and Lafayette, formed its spearhead, shaped its policies and on the whole controlled it; but there were situations and elements which at times could not be controlled. There were between six and seven thousand women in the crowd that set off for Versailles on that wet October day; many of them, doubtless sober, worthy women inspired by some residual belief in the near-divinity of kings; the King had only to be told that one must queue [stand in line] for a whole day to buy a loaf of bread. But there were others who carried broomsticks, skewers and kitchen knives. One woman sharpened her knife on a handy millstone, and said, referring to the Queen, "How glad I should be if I could open up her belly with this knife and tear out her heart." And when two young girls, chosen to represent all, one a flower girl, the other a sculptor's apprentice, had been admitted to the King's presence and emerged without any written promise, but with a report of a kindly reception, they were punched and kicked and, but for intervention, would have been hanged in other women's garters.

Lafayette and the National Guard rode with the crowd and did their best to control it. The King did his best, but the limitations of his understanding are exposed cruelly in his answer to one of the delegates' demand for bread: "I have no bread in my pocket, but you can go to the pantries . . ."

He and his family were forced at last into a carriage and made a slow journey through the rain and the mire to the long-disused palaces of the Tuileries. Damp, dust and spiders had encroached; the young Dauphin said to his mother, "Everything is dirty here, Mama." But Louis, asked what repairs and redecoration he wished for, said, "Let each lodge as he can. I am well enough."

Well enough? Mirabeau for one did not think so. "Do they not see," he wrote to one of the King's friends, "the abyss which is opening at their feet? All is lost; the King and

Queen will perish, and you will see, the mob will tear them limb from limb. You do not fully understand the dangers; nevertheless you must make them see it! . . . If you have any means of inducing the King and Queen to listen to you, persuade them that they and France are doomed if the royal family does not leave Paris.". . .

## Louis' Powers Greatly Diminished

Mirabeau's advice to the King to leave Paris had been rejected, but now, in June 1791, Louis, realizing at last that he had become a puppet, decided to leave the country. The story of the escape of the royal family in disguise from the Tuileries at night, the whole thing arranged by the Queen's Swedish friend, Axel Fersen—the pursuit, the arrest, the dreary, humiliating journey back—has all the quality of melodrama. Even then, being ignominiously hustled back to Paris, Marie Antoinette showed how little she understood the temper of the crowd. She thought that by holding up her young son for the people to see, she could calm them. They were calling her "bitch" and "slut" and "whore"; the gesture evoked more virulent insults, questioning the boy's paternity.

Back in the Tuileries—where some wit had fixed a "To Let" notice on the gate—the nature of their imprisonment became more sinister; formerly it had amounted to little more than what is now known as "house arrest"; now it became stringent. By attempting to flee the country Louis had forfeited much of the people's good will, and somewhere on the road back from Varennes the almost superstitious awe of royalty, which had in the past hedged about and protected kings far more selfish and aggressive, had been lost forever.

The Assembly, still proceeding upon constitutional lines, temporarily suspended all the King's functions.

Louis was stunned to find himself so much hated. To his brother, Provence, who had succeeded in escaping and was busy mustering an army of *émigrés* across the Rhine, he wrote that he had become the slave of his oppressors but that, so long as he was King of France, he would do nothing to dishonor himself. He could have understood it, he said, had he been a Nero [the infamous ancient Roman despot]

. . . but what had he done to be so hated, he who had always cherished the French people who had once loved their kings? The pathetic question answers itself; he was a weak man in a situation where strength was called for. . . .

In September 1791, Louis was restored to his functions and took the oath of fealty to the new Constitution: "I swear to be faithful to the nation and to the law, to use the power which has been delegated to me to maintain the decreed constitution." That power was so diminished as to be virtually non-existent; Louis now held what authority he had from the nation, not by divine right, no longer King of France, but King of the French. . . .

## Threats and Humiliation

To Louis XVI, his brothers' attempt to rouse Europe to come to his rescue had always been embarrassing. The limited power of veto restored to him when he took the oath to

---

### Louis's Last Speech

*In his last public speech, delivered to the Assembly on December 26, 1792, at the conclusion of his trial, Louis impressed many present by managing to maintain his composure and dignity.*

Speaking to you perhaps for the last time I declare to you that my conscience does not reproach me in any way and that my defenders have told you nothing but the truth. I have never feared a public examination of my conduct; but it wounds my heart to find in the indictment the charge that I wished to shed the people's blood, and, above all, that the misfortuncs of 10 August were attributable to me. I confess that the often repeated pledges that I have at all times given of my love for the people and the way in which I have always behaved seem to me an evident proof that I had little fear of endangering myself in order to spare their blood, and that these pledges and this behaviour should preserve me for ever from any such imputation.

Bernard Faÿ, *Louis XVI, or the End of a World.* Translated by Patrick O'Brien. Chicago: Henry Regnery, 1968, p. 397.

the Constitution did not extend to vetoing entry into a war upon which the whole nation was determined. . . .

This war went badly for the French; enthusiasm was no substitute for experience, competent logistics and discipline. When the French were defeated on the Belgian border they murdered not only their prisoners but also their general. In similar fashion, when news of the defeat reached Paris, the Jacobins turned upon the Girondists, and the populace turned upon the King.

At this point Louis' bad judgment and bad luck came into disastrous collision. It was proposed that a camp of 20,000 men should be established near Paris as defense against invasion. This was a matter upon which the King had the right of veto, and he exercised it. The people of Paris drew their own conclusion and stormed the Tuileries. They forced the red cap of liberty on his head. . . .

Then the Duke of Brunswick sent a message: Should the King be harmed, he would destroy Paris. . . . Once again the crowd closed in on the Tuileries. They massacred the loyal Swiss Guards and crowded in the royal apartments from which the King and Queen had just fled, vainly seeking shelter in the Assembly's hall. From there, with their two children and the King's sister, they were taken to genuine imprisonment in the Temple, to be kept under day and night surveillance by ruffianly guards, who delighted to subject them to every possible humiliation.

This violent reaction to a threat from outside had been led by the Jacobins; the Girondists went the way of all moderates in time of crisis; overnight thousands of formerly uncommitted citizens became Jacobins. The King was again suspended from all his functions; the Legislative Assembly was replaced by a National Convention, with all executive power concentrated in the hands of five men, of whom Danton as Minister of Justice was one. . . .

## The Trial

The Convention had already abolished the monarchy and declared France a Republic, "one and indivisible." The King was there, though, alive in his prison, an anachronism and an embarrassing one. Could he be brought to trial? Upon what charges? A commission set to work to find answers to these questions. . . .

The question of what to do with the harmless fat man now known as Louis Capet could not be shelved forever; it cropped up so often and led to such long and heated debates that eventually the Convention was, obliged to impose a limit to the time spent on the subject. The Abbé Gregoire said, "Kings are in the moral order what monsters are in the physical. . . . The history of kings is the martyrology of nations." Young Antoine de Saint-Just, slim and elegant and, despite the fashionable slovenliness, still a dandy, said, "The King must be killed . . . for royalty is an eternal crime . . . the King must not have a long trial . . . he must be killed."

There were many such speeches, but the Convention hesitated. The French are, above all, a logical nation; and there must have been many who, pondering Saint-Just's speech, wondered whether a man born royal and therefore by inference born criminal, should be punished for his crime. In addition those in power had no means of knowing how the country as a whole felt; they feared a Royalist reaction. . . .

Incriminating documents, said to compromise Louis, were found. Robespierre, rapidly attaining ascendancy, said, "Louis cannot be judged because he is already condemned. . . . If he can still be made the cause of a trial he can be acquitted; but if Louis can be presumed innocent what will happen to the revolution?" A tricky, lawyer's question; if Louis were innocent why was he not at Versailles?

The trial began in December 1792. The King made a poor appearance; denied the use of a razor for three days he wore the beginning of a beard on cheeks that now sagged flabbily; his brown coat was shabby. Impartial observers noted that he had not lost his dignity; there still clung about him the ghost, the vanishing shadow of royalty. He had been allowed counsel to defend him . . . but against what? For being born to the throne? Being passive? Being stupid? When the prosecution declared "Louis, the French nation is your accuser," the impersonal nature of the trial was revealed; it was not Louis who was on trial, it was the system of monarchy. . . .

Outside, in the streets, there were Royalist demonstrations. People sang of another King who, abandoned by all but the faithful, had yet been saved. But there was no rallying point for this emotional force, nobody came forward to save *this* King.

## Death of the King

In the Convention one member said, "I am tired of my part of despotism—tormented by the tyranny I am forced to exercise . . ." But Robespierre was there, ready to quell any protest, to stiffen any weakening will.

The verdict was guilty of conspiracy against the national safety. Then for three days the penalty was debated; should Louis be imprisoned, kept in irons or without? Should he be banished? Should he be killed? Tom Paine, the English author of *The Rights of Man*, who, banished from his own country, had come to France and now sat as deputy for the Pas de Calais, voted for imprisonment; but Robespierre was for death, Danton too, and Camille Desmoulins and Marat. . . . There was one vote for death which even to the extremists seemed shocking—that of Louis' cousin . . . now known as Philippe Egalité.

Louis went to the guillotine on January 21, 1793. He made an attempt to address the crowd, "Frenchmen, I die innocent. I pardon the authors of my death. I pray God that the blood about to be spilt will never fall upon the head of France. . . ." Somebody signaled to the drums to resume playing and the rest of his words were drowned. When his head fell, Sanson the executioner lifted it by the hair and displayed it to the crowd.

# The Threat of Defeat and the Reign of Terror

## R.F. Leslie

The Terror, the roughly year-long period in which a small group of radical leaders, most prominent among them Robespierre, wielded almost complete dictatorial power, was in large part a fearful reaction to the imminent threat of defeat by the allied coalition led by Britain, Prussia, and Austria. R.F. Leslie, formerly a history professor at the University of London at Queen Mary College, summarizes that threat; the reaction in Paris, including the rise of Robespierre; the executions in the name of revolutionary justice; and finally the rise of the moderates and fall of the radicals as the dangers to France's armies and borders lessened.

The formidable coalition which was assembled against France in 1793 . . . brought together Russia, Sardinia, Spain, Naples and Sicily, Prussia, Austria, Portugal, the Empire, Baden and the two Hesses in a league against France. Britain was already in alliance with the United Provinces, and George III automatically brought his Electorate of Hanover into the war. The solidarity of the allies was more apparent than real. The sole unifying factor was Great Britain. . . . The official British attitude was the traditional one, that Britain was fighting for the maintenance of the balance of power in Europe. . . . The majority of the states of Europe were concerned neither with ideologies nor principles of action. They were looking simply for opportunities of enlarging their territories. Already even before the formation of the coalition the principle of territorial compensation was under consideration by the continental states. . . .

Reprinted from *The Age of Transformation, 1789 to 1871*, by R.F. Leslie. Copyright 1964 by Blandford Press Ltd. Reprinted by permission.

The war opened in the usual leisurely fashion of the eighteenth-century generals. At once France found herself in a crisis. On 18 March 1793 [Charles] Dumouriez [commander-in-chief of the revolutionary armies] was defeated at the battle of Neerwinden. . . . All the gains of the previous year were now lost and Dumouriez reverted to the policy of combining war with diplomacy. In order to save France from invasion he concluded an armistice with the allied commander, Coburg, which would permit him to lead his troops back into France and overthrow the Convention, but Dumouriez's troops refused to follow him, and on 5 April 1793 he and his staff defected to the Austrians. The allies now had the opportunity to overrun France, but . . . [they] did not pursue the war with vigour. Coburg settled down to a war of sieges in the Low Countries. The Prussians encircled Mainz and the Austrians under Wurmser crossed the Rhine south of Mannheim, but small progress was made. . . . The French were thus able to regroup their forces. The Duke of York was driven back from Dunkirk and Coburg defeated at Hondschoote on 6–8 September and Wattignies on 16 October. The allies made no progress in the south. Lyons fell and the Sardinians were driven back into Savoy. Toulon was besieged and fell to French attack. All that the allies could claim for their efforts in 1793 was that they had recovered the left bank of the Rhine and the Austrian Netherlands and held three French fortresses on the northern frontier of France. They had, however, set in motion within France events which were in startling contrast to the passive generalship of the allies.

## Crisis in the Capital

The desertion of Dumouriez . . . re-created in the minds of the citizens of Paris the uncertainties and fears of August–September 1792 [when anxiety over possible military defeat caused unrest and bloodshed in the capital]. Inflation and the food crisis, coupled with the conviction that France was being betrayed from within, once more produced a revolutionary situation. On 6 April 1793 was created the Committee of Public Safety with the task of supervising the Executive Council. This body was to be elected for one month at a time, and at first the moderate elements predominated. The leading figure in it, Danton, was in effective control of French foreign policy and sought to save France from invasion by conciliation of the opposing powers. On 13 April 1793 by a decree of the Convention it was proclaimed that France would not interfere in the government of other nations. Within France the Committee decided upon a system of price and wage control, to implement which the Decree of the Maximum was issued on 3 May. This was not enough to satisfy the extreme left wing, the so-called Mountain, the deputies who sat upon the upper seats of the Convention. Behind them were the Paris Commune and its sections, demanding a purge of political opponents. On 2 June 1793 the mob and part of the National Guard had appeared before the Tuileries and demanded the arrest of the factious members of the Convention, by whom they meant the Girondins and the Brissotins. The Convention could do no other than submit. The less resolute members departed from Paris and the Jacobins left in control.

## Ruthless Men Take Charge

From July 1793 the composition of the Committee of Public Safety changed. New and ruthless men of great ability now entered it, to form the effective government of France until July 1794. This was not a dictatorship of any one particular member, but the committee certainly exercised the powers of a dictatorial régime. Robespierre, the lawyer from Arras, was perhaps the most prominent member of the Committee and the one whose reputation suffered most at the hands of posterity. He was in fact a man of great personal integrity and like many puritans pushed his purity to extremes, which revolted men with more accommodating moral standards, but he was not alone in the vigour which was now displayed. In effect, the resistance of France depended upon Paris. In the provinces disintegration was everywhere apparent. . . . . Disturbances were evident in Brittany and Normandy. Bordeaux, Marseilles, Lyons and Toulon had rejected the authority of Paris. So low had the credit of the government fallen that in July 1793 the assignat [a paper money bill issued by the revolutionary government] stood at 23 per cent of its face value. The Committee of Public Safety nevertheless was determined to signify to the world that a new epoch had dawned. By a decree of the Convention of 24 November 1793 a new calendar was imposed upon France, reckoned from the autumn equinox of

## Establishing the Committee of Public Safety

*This is the April 6, 1793, decree that created the most powerful and feared of all the revolutionary committees; led by Robespierre and others, it played the major role in the events of the Terror.*

Article 1. A Committee of Public Safety, composed of nine *[later increased to twelve]* members of the National Convention, shall be constituted by roll call.

2. This Committee shall deliberate in secret. It shall be responsible for supervising and accelerating the work of administration entrusted to the Provisional Executive Council whose decrees it may even suspend, when it believes them contrary to the national interest, on condition that it inform the Convention without delay.

3. It is authorized to take, in urgent circumstances, measures for general defence, both internal and external, and its decrees, signed by a majority of members deliberating, which may not be less than two-thirds, shall be executed without delay by the Provisional Executive Council. In no circumstances may it issue arrest warrants, unless against its own executive agents, and on condition that it report thereon to the Convention without delay. . . .

5. Each week it shall make a general written report of its activities and of the condition of the Republic.

6. A register of all its deliberations shall be kept.

7. The Committee is established for a month only.

8. The National Treasury shall remain independent of the executive committee and subject to the immediate oversight of the Convention, in the manner established by decree.

D.I. Wright, ed., *The French Revolution: Introductory Documents*. St. Lucia: University of Queensland Press, 1974, pp. 154–55.

1792, from which the year I began, with months each with names to indicate its character. The very introduction of this calendar was an indication that the republican régime was confident that it could make itself the master of France and impose upon the country its own enlightenment.

In some manner governmental authority in France had to be restored. The assassination of the left-wing journalist, Marat, by Charlotte Corday pointed the way to a drastic political purge. The revolutionary Tribunal established in Paris began to increase the number of political trials. Under the Law of the Suspects of 17 September 1793 virtually any opponent of the regime could be arrested, and many were given a summary trial and executed upon the guillotine. The most famous victim was the queen, Marie Antoinette, but with her died many of the prominent figures of the early stage of the revolution, Brissot, Vergniaud, the Duke of Orleans, called Philippe Égalité for his support of the revolution, Madame Du Barry and the scientist Lavoisier. Others anticipated conviction and death by suicide, Roland, Condorcet, Clavière and Pétion. In the March of 1794 the extreme left in Paris, Hébert and his followers, most famous for their anticlericalism and institution of the Cult of Reason, were executed, but in April Danton and the relatively moderate group around him met the same fate. In the end the Committee of Public Safety represented nothing except itself. It enjoyed no basis of popular support. While France was under threat of invasion the Committee, by the law of 4 Frimaire Year II (4 December 1793) in control of all subordinate authorities in France, achieved a degree of centralization beyond the dreams of the Bourbon monarchs and held France together by the exercise of the political purge which has come to have the name of the Terror. Perhaps as many as 300,000 persons were arrested, but far fewer were executed. . . .

## The Moderates Raise Their Heads

The horror of the Terror should not be allowed to detract from the very real achievements of the Committee of Public Safety. In October 1793 Lyons fell to the Republican Army and the internal discords vanished before the onslaught of the government. An army of 650,000 men was created, officered by young men who under the Old Régime could never have found expression for their ability. Pichegru, Masséna, Moreau, Davout, Lefèvre, Serrurier, Augerau, Brune and, not least, Bonaparte [all skilled army officers] appeared to give force and renewed vigour to a system of warfare which had in the eighteenth century developed the finesse of a game of chess and lost sight of the fact that battles have a wider strategic purpose. The war which the French Revolution was prepared to fight was not one of set battles and compromise peace, but a struggle for total victory. Total victory, however, or even the partial victory of French arms spelled defeat for the dedicated Left, which ruled in Paris. On 26 June 1794 the French army defeated the allies at the battle of Fleurus and once more the Austrian Netherlands were overrun by French troops. The internal revolts were suppressed or rendered ineffective. The danger to France had passed and the need for severity had gone. Now the moderates raised their heads. The left wing in the Committee of Public Safety had rendered their service to France and public anxiety subsided. Robespierre and his followers wished to maintain the momentum of the Revolution. On 26 July 1794 Robespierre denounced the enemies of the Revolution in the Convention and stirred his opponents into resistance. On 27 July the moderates summoned their courage and attacked Robespierre. By a vote of the Convention Robespierre and his supporters were arrested before they could summon their supporters from the streets of Paris. On the following day Robespierre, Saint Just, Couthon, Hanriot and seventeen others were executed. The Paris Commune was purged of its left-wing element and the capital freed from the violence and the high idealism of the proletarian revolution. These events which took place between the 8th and 10th of the revolutionary month of Thermidor are known as the Thermidorian Reaction. Undoubtedly the inhabitants of France could breathe a sigh of relief, but the rule of the Terror has served ever since as an example of what ruthless centralization can obtain for a revolution. In the future men were to look back to the France of 1793–94 for a model of what a revolution could achieve in the face of apparently overwhelming odds.

# The Revolutionary Army and the Rise of Napoléon Bonaparte

Martyn Lyons

An associate professor of history at the University of New South Wales in Australia and a prolific writer on the French Revolution, Martyn Lyons discusses the attitude of the French Directory toward its military generals. Trusting neither their political loyalties nor personal ambitions, at first the politicians tried to limit their power. In time, however, the Directory became dependent on its generals, a reality that allowed Napoléon to enhance his own reputation in the government's service and ultimately at its expense. Lyons concentrates on Napoléon's Italian campaigns, his treaty with Austria, and his largely unsuccessful Egyptian expedition, ending with his return to France, which would soon see his successful political coup and acquisition of dictatorial power.

The French Revolution had always been wary of its generals. Ever since the emigration of many royalist army officers between 1789 and 1791, the political loyalties of France's military leadership were closely scrutinised. The Republic attempted to make the army subservient to the politicians but during the régime of the Directory (1795–99), Bonaparte established a wide sphere of independence for himself. He commanded the army of Italy as a loyal republican but his success enhanced his own reputation rather than that of the ailing Directory. The Italian campaign did not only make

Bonaparte an illustrious commander, it also transformed him into a figure of political importance in European affairs.

## Trying to Keep the Generals in Line

There were very good reasons why the Revolution had tried to keep its generals under close surveillance. Their personal ambitions had frequently threatened to undermine political stability. Lafayette had defected to the Prussians after the Revolution of 10 August 1792, taking twenty-two members of his general staff with him. Then, in 1793, General Dumouriez had defected to the Austrians after failing to launch a military coup against Paris. Generals who failed to deliver the victories the Republic needed were dismissed and could be accused of treason.

The best guarantee against military dictatorship was to politicise the troops themselves. *Sans-culotte* recruits were not blindly obedient foot soldiers; they were quick to criticise and denounce the deficiencies of their commanders. General Dillon had even been shot by his own troops during a retreat near Lille in 1792. Another method of maintaining civilian control over the army was to appoint civilian *commissaires des guerres* (war commissars) to the armies, who could report disloyalty and incompetence to Paris. In Italy, however, Bonaparte's *commissaires* were his allies. They included his Corsican colleague, Saliceti.

The Republican army offered rapid promotion to talented and ambitious individuals. Deaths, emigration and dismissals opened up new avenues for social advancement. Many soldiers, besides Bonaparte himself, rose to high positions at a comparatively young age, in a sphere where the principle of the career open to talent seemed to be a spectacular reality. [Louis-Lazare] Hoche, for example, son of an ostler [horse or mule keeper], was a general at the age of 26, and [Pierre François] Augereau, the son of a fruiterer, emerged from humble origins to become a general in his thirties.

The Directory tried to keep its generals at arm's length. Augereau, for example, was twice a candidate for election as a Director, but was twice unsuccessful. In the Year 5, however, the army made a decisive intervention in domestic politics. The elections of Fructidor Year 5 (1797) produced the result that the republican government most feared: a royalist majority was returned. Afraid for the stability of the régime, the Directory annulled the elections in forty-nine departments and called in Augereau's forces to disperse the deputies. On the night of 17 Fructidor, troops of the 17th division occupied the legislative chambers and arrested royalist sympathisers. Fifty-three deputies became victims of the "dry guillotine"—in other words, they were deported. The survival of the Republic was guaranteed, but at a huge price. The Constitution of the Year 3 had been violated, the electoral process devalued, and the régime was now indebted to the army. Bonaparte was to be the ultimate beneficiary of the process of change set in motion by the coup of Fructidor. The constitution was increasingly discredited and the Directory was becoming dangerously dependent on its generals. This dependency was exploited by Bonaparte in the brilliant Italian campaign of 1796–97.

## The Invasion of Italy

Italy was a patchwork of tiny states, divided by long-standing municipal rivalries and exploited for centuries as a battleground for the great European powers. The Kingdom of Sardinia, which ruled over Piedmont from its capital in Turin, guarded the Alpine passes. The Milanais was a dominion of the Austrian Habsburgs and fossilised oligarchies ruled the ancient republics of Genoa and Venice. . . . Austria was the dominant power in the Italian peninsula which it defended from the northern system of fortresses, known as the Quadrilateral, and consisting of Mantua, Verona, Peschiera and Legnago. Austrian influence was strong south of the river Po in the miniature duchies of Parma, Piacenza and Modena, as well as in Tuscany. . . .

In Italy, therefore, France could strike at the power of its arch enemy, Austria, as well as limiting British Mediterranean sea power. The valuables and art treasures stored in the churches and courts of Italy also attracted a régime which still faced acute financial difficulties. Bonaparte urged the government to authorise an advance on Turin and then the

Milanais, to separate the Sardinian and Austrian forces. The Directory, he argued in a note of 29 Nivose Year 4, should give its commander (himself, he hoped) plenty of scope . . . because speed was of the essence. . . .

Bonaparte was persuasive, and in March 1796 he was appointed to lead the army of Italy, only 50,000 strong. The Directory's efforts, however, were focused principally on the Rhine and the government did not envisage the degree of commitment to the Italian sphere which followed. Bonaparte married Joséphine and arrived in Nice. . . . His generals found him a very unimposing figure, and did not know what to make of the clumsy new arrival who insisted on showing everybody his wife's portrait. He was a Corsican and had been an associate of terrorists. He had helped to clear the streets of Paris of royalists . . . but that was hardly comparable to the experience of real warfare. Doubters were soon to be disabused. On 27 March, he made a proclamation to his ill-fed troops. . . . "Soldiers, you are naked and hungry", he later claimed to have said.

> The government owes you much, but can give you nothing. I am about to lead you into the world's most fertile plains. Rich provinces and great cities will be in your power, and in them you will find honour, glory, and riches. Soldiers of Italy, why should you want for courage and steadfastness? . . .

Bonaparte fulfilled his promise. He divided the forces of his enemies and defeated the Sardinians in the series of engagements known as the Battle of Mondovi. . . . An armistice was signed with Sardinia at Cherasco and the French pressed on to Milan, which they occupied in May 1796. French success in both Piedmont and Lombardy was aided by the activities of Italian Jacobins, who saw in the French a hope for liberal government and progress towards a unified Italy. Their hopes, as we shall see, were to be disappointed, but for a time it suited the French to encourage them. . . .

## Making His Own Policy

The Austrians, however, were not defeated; they had withdrawn to their defences in the Quadrilateral. The Directory ordered Bonaparte to advance no further against Austria, but to concentrate on the subordination and plunder of central Italy. But Bonaparte was soon in a position to determine his own policy. . . .

Bonaparte paid his troops in cash instead of in *assignats*, the discredited paper currency of the Revolution, which helped to establish his personal control over the army of Italy. Otherwise, the conduct of the campaign thus far was entirely consistent with the aims of the Directory in Paris. He was careful to behave as a loyal servant of the Republic. After Cherasco, he laid the captured flags of the enemy before the Republican government. He willingly complied with the government's explicit directives to seek out valuable art treasures. The transport of such works to Paris would "repair the ravages of vandalisim" during the Revolution, and ensure France's rightful "supremacy in art". . . . By the end of 1796, 46 million francs had been mulcted [looted] from Italy, not to mention priceless art works. Bonaparte himself pocketed 3 million francs, much of which was distributed to members of his large and needy family network.

Paris approved of all this, but the creation of an independent Cispadane Republic (= south of the river Po), comprising Modena and the Legations, was not on the government's agenda. Formed in Reggio (Emilia) in January 1797, the Cispadane adopted the Italian version of the tricolour, the red, white and green which were to become the national colours. The Directory, however, was reluctant to enter into the long-term commitment of supporting sister or satellite Republics. Italy, in the Directory's thinking, could help to finance the war and provide bargaining counters when the Rhine frontier was to be negotiated. An independent Bonapartist policy, however, was emerging, over which Paris had little control. The French became even more deeply embroiled in Italy when the Cisalpine Republic was created, uniting the Cispadane with Lombardy and Bergamo, with its capital in Milan. . . .

## Bonaparte's Double Victory

The Austrians had retreated to the Quadrilateral and the French army, weakened by exhaustion and casualties, took months to beat them back. . . . Eventually, French victories at Arcole and Rivoli in the winter of 1796–97 forced the Austrians to abandon the fortress of Mantua. Having dislodged the Austrians from their stronghold, Bonaparte marched into the Tyrol, disobeying instructions once again, and forced an armistice at Leoben, only eighty miles from Vienna, on 29 Germinal Year 5. The terms of the armistice were to be consolidated in the Treaty of Campoformio in the Year 6.

In these diplomatic negotiations, Bonaparte asserted his own version of French foreign policy and presented the outcome to the Directory as a *fait accompli* [done deal]. He forced the Austrians to accept his Cisalpine Republic, offering them compensation in Venice. In Paris, the Director Reubell was appalled. Bonaparte had committed France too deeply in Italy and the all-important problem of the Rhineland had been shelved. . . . Many interpreted the French failure to insist on territorial security in Germany as a feeble surrender to Austria.

This was hardly the view that the Austrians themselves took of Campoformio. Vienna had lost Belgium, Lombardy, the Papal Legations and Mantua. These severe losses left the Habsburgs powerless to prevent the spread of Republicanism in the Italian peninsula. . . . Bonaparte's orientation of French policy towards a new Mediterranean dimension condemned the whole of Europe to a continuation of the war.

Campoformio was a triumph for Bonaparte. The Directory, divided within itself, could not argue with a general who delivered such spectacular victories and war booty. They reluctantly accepted his decisions. . . . The Directory had failed to secure peace with England or an alliance with Prussia, and peace on Bonaparte's terms was popular in France. It was a fragile and a transient peace but it brought the First Coalition against France to an end. It made Bonaparte a continental statesman as well as a military commander and, for him, this constituted a double victory: that of the French over the Austrians, and that of Bonaparte over the civilian government.

## The Egyptian Expedition

The Directory's attempts to weaken or defeat Britain had proved abortive. An expedition had left Brest in 1796 to invade Ireland, but bad weather and indifferent navigation had prevented it from reaching its destination. A further plan to send a fleet across the English Channel was judged too risky. Attention shifted to Egypt, where France could inhibit British trade and sea power, and cut the route to India. Egypt could also perhaps provide France with cotton, rice and coffee in compensation for her lost Caribbean possessions. Egypt was dominated by the warrior élite of Mamelukes, 50,000-strong, originally imported by the Turks from the Caucasus. If the expedition could turn the population against the Mamelukes, the Ottoman Empire might be enticed into an alliance.

The Egyptian expedition offered Bonaparte further scope for his talents and inevitably revived the coalition against France. The Directory, it is often thought, was happy to get rid of Bonaparte, whose success and personal ambitions were a political embarrassment. But this was hardly a good reason for risking an experienced army so far afield, across seas patrolled by the Royal Navy. It is more likely that Bonaparte wanted to put distance between himself and the Directory. In Egypt he would be free of political supervision and the attention of civilian war commissars. There he could pose as a modern Alexander and become a statesman on a grand intercontinental scale. . . .

The Egypt expedition has been seen as the first example of modern orientalism, a European encounter with the Islamic east, in which the abilities of scholars and intellectuals were harnessed for an imperialist purpose. To "know" Egypt, to record it, draw its pyramids, study its agriculture and social arrangements were as much expressions of colonial domination as the presence of the French army. To chart the land and define its resources were synonymous with subordinating it and making it into an extension of French learning. The twenty-three volumes of the *Description de l'Egypte*, published between 1809 and 1828, were perhaps the most lasting result of the Egypt expedition, and an important contribution to the subjugation of the east by western imperialism.

The Battle of the Nile, on 1 August 1798, in which [British admiral Horatio] Nelson's fleet finally located the French at anchor in Aboukir Bay, and destroyed it, made lasting success in Egypt impossible. Nevertheless, Bonaparte set about defeating the Mamelukes and attempting, by his benevolent administration, to win Moslem cooperation. "We are the friends of true Moslems" he told the people of Alexandria and he insisted that the French should respect Islamic conventions. . . . He ruled Egypt with characteristic pragmatism, but there were limits to his wish to placate local leaders. The French could not be accepted as "true Moslems" unless they accepted both circumcision and the religious ban on the consumption of alcohol. Not even a Bonaparte could demand such sacrifices from a French army. The French levied taxes, which were collected by the Coptic minority, and confiscated the property of the defeated Mamelukes. Windmills were introduced to grind flour and the irrigation system was improved. French coinage was introduced and a hospital founded. . . .

Without naval support Bonaparte's options were limited. In 1799, he marched on Syria, hoping to force Turkey out of the coalition against France. He took Jaffa, where 2,000 were slaughtered by the French. Many prisoners were killed because the French did not have enough supplies to feed them. Bonaparte was then held up for two months at St. John of Acre by Djezzar Pasha, whose *jihad* (holy war) against the French was supported by a squadron of the Royal Navy. Plague began to reduce French forces, and in May 1798 Bonaparte was compelled to retreat. . . . Perhaps less than one half of the 10,000 troops who invaded Syria returned alive.

By now news had reached Bonaparte of French military defeats in Europe and a developing political crisis in Paris. These events called him back to France, and a new political role. On 6 Fructidor (24 August 1799), Bonaparte abandoned his army, evaded the British naval blockade and sailed for home.

Chapter 3

# Social and Cultural Aspects of the Revolution

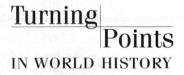

Turning Points

IN WORLD HISTORY

# How the Revolution's Divorce Laws Affected Private Life

Lynn Hunt

Major changes in the institution of marriage, and in particular the process of divorce, constituted one of the clearest examples of the French revolutionary government's attempt to create a new, more liberal and enlightened society. Lynn Hunt, of the University of Pennsylvania, a noted translator and scholar of the Revolution, suggests that government leaders tried to achieve a balance among individual rights, traditional family bonds, and state control. Divorce became relatively easy, partly because it was inexpensive, and also because the new laws provided many possible grounds for ending a marriage. Significantly, the divorce process was open equally to men and women, befitting the revolutionary ideal of the equality of all citizens before the law. This situation changed later, under Napoléon's dictatorship, which imposed much tighter restrictions on freedom of marriage and divorce.

In no domain was the invasion of public authority more evident [during the Revolution] than in family life. Marriage was secularized, and the ceremony, to be considered binding, had to be performed before a municipal official. Under the ancien régime marriage was formalized by the exchange of consent from the two parties; the priest was only a witness to the exchange. By the far-reaching decree of 20 September 1792, the official not only had charge of the civil registers but also declared the couple united in the eyes of the law. Public

Reprinted by permission of the publisher from Lynn Hunt, "The Unstable Boundaries of the French Revolution," in *A History of Private Life*, vol. 4, *From the Fires of Revolution to the Great War*, edited by Michelle Perrot, Cambridge, Mass.: Harvard University Press. Copyright ©1990 by the President and Fellows of Harvard College.

authority was now taking an active part in the formation of the family. The state determined the obstacles to marriage; reestablished and regulated the process of adoption; accorded rights (severely restricted under the civil code) to illegitimate children; instituted divorce; and limited parental powers. By attempting to establish a new national system of education, the National Convention proceeded on the principle that children, as Danton said, "belong to the Republic before they belong to their parents." Bonaparte himself insisted that "the law takes the child at birth, provides for his education, prepares him for a profession, regulates how and under what conditions he can marry, travel, and choose a profession."

The legislation on family life demonstrates the competing concerns of the revolutionary governments. The protection of individual liberty, the maintenance of family solidarity, and the consolidation of state control had to be balanced. During the period of the National Convention, in particular, though even earlier, the revolutionary state gave priority to the protection of individuals against the possible tyranny of family and church. . . . Nevertheless, with the institution of family courts in August 1790, the legislators encouraged family resolution of disputes between family members, including eventually divorce (made possible by another law promulgated on 20 September 1792). The Civil Code was far less preoccupied with the happiness and autonomy of the individual, especially of women, emphasizing the powers of the father. The powers attributed to the family courts were either restored to the father as head of the family or taken over by state courts. In general, the state often limited family or church control only in order to increase its own; it guaranteed individual rights, encouraged family solidarity, and limited parental powers.

## The Right to Divorce

The tension between individual rights, family maintenance, and state control is very marked in the case of divorce, which was instituted for the first time in French history during the Revolution. Divorce was the logical consequence of the liberal ideas expressed in the Constitution of 1791. Article 7 had secularized marriage: "The law henceforth regards marriage only as a civil contract." If marriage was a civil contract based on consent, it could be broken. Such reasoning was given further impetus by the force of circumstances. The Civil Constitution of the Clergy had divided the Catholic Church, and in many communes couples were refusing to take marriage vows before a *jureur* (clergyman who had taken the oath of allegiance to the government). By secularizing marriage, the state gained control over the civil registers (births, deaths, marriages) and replaced the church as the ultimate authority in questions of family life. In debates over divorce, which, despite the novelty of the proposed law, were not very extensive, other reasons for instituting divorce were cited: relief for the unhappy couple; the liberation of women from marital despotism; and freedom of conscience for Protestants and Jews, because the religion of these groups did not proscribe divorce.

The divorce law of 1792 was remarkably liberal. Seven grounds for divorce were admitted: insanity; conviction for crimes entailing corporal punishment or loss of civil rights; crimes, brutality, or grave injury inflicted by one partner on the other; notorious dissoluteness of morals; abandonment for at least two years; absence without news for at least five years; emigration (when taken as a sign of counterrevolutionary intentions). In such cases, divorce was granted immediately. In addition, a couple could divorce by mutual consent with at most a four-month delay, and divorce was granted also for incompatibility of temperament or character after a six-month period of attempted reconciliation. A one-year wait was required before remarriage. The judicial procedures involved were so inexpensive that divorce was available to most of the population; most strikingly, it was available to both women and men on equal terms. At that time it was the most liberal law anywhere in the world.

Under Title VI of the Napoleonic Civil Code, the number of grounds for divorce was reduced to three: conviction for crimes entailing corporal punishment or loss of civil rights; brutality; or adultery. In line with Napoleon's general reaffirmation of paternal powers, the rights of women were severely curtailed. The husband could seek divorce on the basis of his wife's adultery, but the wife could only request divorce if her husband "kept his concubine in their family home" (article 230). Moreover, if she was convicted of adultery, she was liable to two years imprisonment, while he escaped any punishment. Divorce by mutual consent was maintained, but with many restrictions: the husband had to be at least twenty-five years old; the wife between twenty-one and forty-five years of age; the length of the marriage had to be between two and twenty years duration; and parental permission had to be obtained. There were some 30,000 divorces in France between 1792 and 1803, but many fewer afterward (divorce was abolished in 1816). In Lyons, to take an example that has been closely studied, there were 87 divorces a year between 1792 and 1804, and only 7 a year between 1805 and 1816. In Rouen, 43 percent of the 1,129 divorces between 1792 and 1816 were granted between 1792 and 1795; after 1803 there were only 6 divorces granted a year.

## The Impact of Liberal Divorce Laws

Did the possibility of divorce have a real impact on the private lives of the new citizens of the Republic? In the cities, certainly, but far less so in the countryside. In Toulouse, for example, there were 347 divorces between 1792 and 1803, but in the rural districts of Revel and Muret there were only 2 each during the same period. In the big cities such as Lyons and Rouen, as many as 3–4 percent of the marriages contracted during the Revolution had been broken by divorce by 1802—within at most ten years of marriage. Around 1900, after the reinstitution of divorce in 1884, the divorce rate was 6.5 percent—probably not much higher than the rate of the 1790s, given that divorce was readily available only during the ten years after 1792. Divorced couples came from all strata of urban society, though artisans, merchants, and professionals may have divorced somewhat more often. Women apparently benefited from the new laws; in two-thirds of the cases in Lyons and Rouen brought by one or the other spouse (not mutual consent), the proceedings were initiated by women. Divorce was not often based on mutual consent: in only one out of four or five cases did the couple seek a divorce jointly.

The primary causes of divorce under the 1792 law were abandonment or prolonged absence. The next most-cited cause was incompatibility. Even the driest statistics tell a sad story on occasion: one-quarter of those citing abandonment in Lyons complained that the absence of a spouse had lasted ten years or more! Fully half of the spouses had been gone five years or more. The Revolution offered some the occasion to bring the legal situation in line with reality. And that reality included some perennial problems. Men and women cited abandonment and incompatibility in nearly equal numbers as their reason for seeking a divorce, but are we surprised to learn that women were much more likely to complain of brutality? The records of the family courts and later the civil courts are filled with stories of husbands assaulting their wives, often on returning home from the cabaret, with fists, brooms, crockery, fire irons, and sometimes even knives.

Divorce legislation was not intended simply to liberate the individual from the constraints of an unhappy domestic situation. The unhappy couple had to work out the divorce arrangements through a family court or a family meeting, depending on the kind of divorce requested. These were composed of relatives (or friends if relatives were lacking), chosen by the husband and wife to decide the merits of the case and property settlements and child custody. Divorce was apparently quite readily accepted, since only one-third to one-half of the petitions for divorce were dropped (presumably in part because of family pressure). The number of cases pursued to completion is surprising, given the novelty of divorce and the church's resistance to it. Even most constitutional bishops only accepted divorce on the condition that it not lead to remarriage during the lifetime of the other spouse. Nevertheless, about one-fourth of the men and women who obtained divorces remarried. (After 1816 the church accepted these remarriages if the original marriages had been secular ones, on the grounds that such marriages had no validity.) Petitions for divorce rarely led to custody battles—partly because many of those seeking divorce had no underage children (three-fifths of the divorcing couples in Lyons and Rouen had no minor children), and partly because neither the courts nor the parents seemed to consider children an integral part of the family unit. Evidence for the latter, though largely negative, is nonetheless convincing: children were rarely cited in the depositions of the couple or in court records; the decisions made for the custody of children were rarely if ever disputed; and frequently the couple mentioned that they had children, without giving their names or even, on occasion, the number of them in the family.

## A Window into Private Life

Divorce proceedings provide one of the few windows onto private sensibility during the Revolution. It is not clear how much changed in the affective life of the individual during this troubled time. P.J.B. Nougaret [a leading songwriter of the Revolution] tells the story of a daughter made pregnant by her married lover. Her mother pretends to be pregnant so that they can go off to the country until the daughter gives birth, thus protecting the daughter's honor. This exemplary mother in *Paris ou le rideau levé* (published in Year VIII) seems untouched by the revolutionary experience. The problems experienced in marital relations were probably much the same as they had been before 1789. The Revolution certainly did not invent wife-beating. But the very possibility of divorce must have had some influence on marriage. Now there were women, such as the Lyonnaise Claudine Ramey, who wanted to leave her husband because "she could not be happy with him." For many, love had to be the foundation of marriage. And marriage itself seemed to enjoy an unusual vogue during the Revolution; the average annual number of marriages jumped from 239,000 under Louis XVI to 327,000 in 1793. Not all of these were for love alone; the proportion of marriages in which the husband was less than twenty-five years old and ten years younger than his wife grew from 9–10 to 19 percent in 1796—probably because marriage was the best means of avoiding conscription.

# The Revolution Versus the Church

Emmet Kennedy

The leaders of the Revolution saw the Catholic Church as a monolithic institution that only perpetuated the divisions and inequalities of the country's old regime. In their reorganized France, the church became, in effect, part of the state, subject to state rules; one of the most controversial of these rules was the requirement that members of the clergy recite an oath of loyalty to the government and people. In this highly informative essay, Emmet Kennedy, professor of history at George Washington University, tells how the state's attack on the church divided France along religious/secular lines and created social discord rather than harmony.

The revolutionary attack on the Catholic church in France began with the attack on feudalism. . . . On 4 August 1789 the men of the National, or Constituent, Assembly (created in consequence of the Tennis Court Oath of 20 June) abolished feudalism and the privileges not only of seigneurs [lords] but also of provinces, municipalities, officeholders, and the church, which lost a principal means of support—the tithe [a proportion of a person's yearly income paid to help support the church]. Fiscal equality and equality of opportunity replaced privilege. When all privileges, which erected so many intermediary powers between crown and subject, were abolished, there remained only the individual, invested with sacred rights, and the nation, invested with the equally sacred authority of the "general will," specifically invoked in the declaration.

Reprinted by permission of the publisher from *A Cultural History of the French Revolution*, by Emmet Kennedy (New Haven: Yale University Press, 1989). Copyright 1989 by Emmet Kennedy.

## The Church Becomes an Organ of Government

The long-term reasons for the attack on the church included
. . . egalitarianism (rights of priests vis-à-vis bishops) . . . rationalism and utilitarianism, popular antipathy to clerical tax
exemptions and the tithe, and resentment over the moral
failings of clerics. The "good conscience" of 1789 wanted
the church to be purer, poorer, more apostolic, more responsive to the indigent, and more removed from the court
and aristocracy.

Confiscation of church property (2 November 1789), unlike the suppression of the tithe, did not stem from popular
discontent with the church. Few of the 1789 general *cahiers*,
or statements of grievances, collected in the *bailliages* and
*sénéchaussées* (electoral districts) demanded confiscation. Besides, the Declaration of Rights had declared property a sacred right (article 17). How, then, did the confiscation come
about?

Both Mirabeau, the principal orator of the Constituent
Assembly, and [Charles Maurice de] Talleyrand [bishop of
Autun, who represented the second estate at the Estates
General], its most influential cleric, charged by the finance
committee to float a loan, believed that since the assembly
had abolished one source of ecclesiastical revenue (the tithe)
another had to be found. Church property, Talleyrand argued, was different from that of private citizens, since the
church merely held it in trust for such public purposes as divine worship, charitable works, and education. If the state
could provide these services, the intention of the benefactors
who contributed the property could be honored. On 2 November 1789, the assembly voted 568 to 346 in favor of
Mirabeau's proposal to put the property of the clergy at the
disposition of the nation. The French church, now merely
an organ of government, had ceased to be independent. The
distinction between church and state, which originated with
Western Christianity . . . was eclipsed by a more "ancient
liberty." In this rediscovered pagan liberty, the Christian dualism of the spiritual and the temporal would disappear before the absolute dominion of the temporal.

## Religious Emancipation in Stages

The Enlightenment made universal tolerance and the brotherhood of all men the centerpiece of a new order—"a party of humanity." Before the Revolution, Protestants had no legal right to hold public office (Louis XVI's most famous minister, Jacques Necker, was excepted because he was a foreigner). . . . The edict of 1787, which the government of Louis XVI passed in the face of opposition by the clergy and parlements, recognized Protestant marriages but required that they be validated before a judge or priest. Fewer than half the general cahiers that broached the issue approved of tolerance, whereas 60 percent (weighted heavily by the clergy) wished to maintain Catholicism as "the only public cult." The deputies of 1789 tried to satisfy both constituencies. Article 10 of the Declaration of the Rights of Man and Citizen stated: "No one may be disturbed on account of his opinions, even religious ones, provided they do not disturb the public order established by the law." The following article assured "free communication of thoughts and opinions" by speech and by the written or printed word. Law would restrict only abuses. Yet before the Terror, no official measures were taken to disestablish or separate the Catholic church from the state. . . .

It would seem that Catholicism was recognized de facto as the paramount but not sole religion of the French. The idea that all men are "born free and equal in rights" and that "liberty consists in the power to do whatever does not harm another" (articles 1 and 4 of the declaration) included religious liberty. Such liberty was grounded in the recent theory of natural law, which spoke of individual rights as claims against society and the state. The part of the natural law that spoke of obligations was played down in the 1789 text and would not reappear until after Thermidor, and then strictly in a social rather than a religious context.

For both Protestants and Jews, emancipation came in stages. After the limited liberty granted to Protestants in 1787, a decree of January 1789 gave them the electoral franchise, which they used to elect fifteen deputies to the Estates

General, among them Rabaut Saint-Etienne from Montauban. On 24 December Protestants were made eligible for any public office. . . .

In 1784 Louis XVI suppressed a personal tax . . . on Jews. . . . But continuing hostility toward Jews was expressed in the cahiers of 1789. In December 1789, the assembly discussed civil rights for non-Catholics. Robespierre spoke of expiating crimes against the Jews perpetrated by France and other nations. "How can the social interest of society be founded on the violation of eternal principles of justice and of reason, which are the foundations of any human society?" But the proposal to grant Jews equal civic rights was postponed. In September 1791, after interventions by Mirabeau . . . and radical journalists like Antoine-Joseph Gorsas, . . . the assembly granted civic rights to those Jews who would take an oath of loyalty to the constitution. This oath was administered simultaneously to other categories of Frenchmen, such as clergy and teachers. Emancipation came for the Sephardic Jews of the south in January 1790. Granting civil liberties to Protestants and Jews was less a sign of Christian tolerance than an indication of the secularization of French state and society, which no longer could be called officially Catholic. The new communitarian bond was the nation rather than the church; it was no longer necessary to belong to the church to belong fully to the nation.

## The Church Reorganized on Civil Lines

On 13 February 1790, following a law abolishing religious vows the previous autumn, all religious orders—except those performing teaching or such other useful public services as hospital care—were dissolved. Vows of perpetual obedience, poverty, and chastity appeared to the men of 1789 to violate the inalienable rights of personal freedom embodied in the Declaration of Rights, just as monasteries violated its anticorporate ideology. . . .

The exodus from the monasteries was often followed by active engagement in new careers opened up by the Revolution. Following the philosophes' hostility to celibacy, the

Legislative Assembly resolved that marriage, since it was of natural law, was compatible with the priesthood. (That marriage was not an obligation of natural law seems to have eluded the legislators.) It went on to say "that the law no longer recognizes either religious vows, nor any other engagement, which would be contrary to natural law and to the constitution, that the quality of French citizen has lost any affiliation with any corporation which demands religious vows." Religion was henceforth to exist entirely within the confines of the civil order of society, of which marriage was a "primary unit," whereas celibacy was a condition fit only for a transcendental order.

The Civil Constitution of the Clergy, voted by the assembly on 12 July 1790, helped simultaneously to disorganize the French Catholic church and establish a new church tied to the state. Since clerical salaries now depended on the state, the state necessarily intervened in the church's internal organization. The number of parishes was to be reduced, and dioceses were made coterminous with the eighty-three new *départements* (provincial administrative districts) that divided up the old *généralités*. Both priests and bishops were to be chosen by the electorate—that is, the active (propertied) citizens who voted in civil elections. Those not paying the minimal property tax were excluded, but non-Catholics and nonpracticing Catholics who met the property qualifications could vote. The state was defining the religious *ecclesia* by civil criteria, substituting the democratic principle of sovereignty for the Catholic apostolic succession. The Gallican precedent, whereby the king nominated many of France's abbots and bishops (who were then canonically instated by the pope), was being extended beyond recognition. As the bishop of Aix put it during debate on this issue on 29 May 1790: "We are certainly astonished to see disappear in this way the holy canons and title deeds of the Church. . . . It is possible for some retrenchments to be made in the Church; but the Church must be consulted." The church was not consulted. Article 19 of the constitution went so far as to forbid a bishop to communicate with Rome for confirmation of his appointment. . . .

## The Oath of Loyalty

To convince themselves and the public of their rectitude and of the legitimacy of their actions, the revolutionaries stressed the compatibility of old and new. Popular sovereignty was proclaimed, but the king was to remain king. And although the church was dispossessed and reorganized unilaterally without Rome's consent, everyone who approved it insisted that it was in union with Rome in matters of doctrine. . . .

Such euphoria could not conceal the cleavages among the French caused by revolutionary legislation. An oath of November 1790 to the Civil Constitution of the Clergy was required of all ecclesiastics. The clergy, far from unanimously supporting the new measures, was sorely divided. Only 7 of 160 bishops took the new oath, which read: "I swear to be faithful to the nation, to the law and the king, and to maintain with all my power the Constitution determined by the National Assembly and accepted by the king." Since an integral part of the new but still incomplete constitution would be the Civil Constitution of the Clergy, bishops, who were well versed in canon law and responsible to the pope for both their office and tenure, could not be expected to approve it. Almost all bishops were noble, which perhaps made them less disposed to accept democracy in the church.

The overall rate of acceptance of the regular clergy (those belonging to religious orders) has not been tabulated completely, but figures for Paris show a weakening of resistance as the Revolution progressed. Some 468 of 916 religious records remain. Of these 468 clerics, 33 percent took the oath by 1791, 45 percent by 1792, 54 percent by the time of the Terror, and 62 percent by 1796–97. . . .

The confused laity resented illegitimate pastors and often challenged their right to dispense sacraments. The authorities, for their part, took forceful measures to install those who swore to the constitution. Little by little, they prevented those who refused the oath, the "refractory" clergy, from practicing. Attempts to explain why certain . . . vicars took the oath and others refused have not produced simple answers. Economic considerations may have motivated some clergy. . . .

The level of education also may have influenced clerics' choice. In rural areas no pattern is evident, but in towns, where clergy tended to refuse the oath in larger proportions than in the countryside, many clerics had university degrees. These educated urban clergy may have been more aware than their rural counterparts of the conflict between the principles of the Enlightenment and the Revolution and those of the church. Oath-taking must ultimately be seen as a consequence of the new religious liberty enunciated by the Declaration of Rights. . . .

## The Nation Divided

The Revolution, which had begun by removing all religious barriers to create one nation, had managed to erect a formidable divide that set many of the French against the Revolution. A spate of catechisms sought to sway Catholics to one side or the other. The Catholic catechisms stressed the unity . . . that marked the church. Schism was "the greatest of all the crimes," and those who perpetrated it were "ravishing wolves." The assembly's civil jurisdiction was acknowledged, but not its ecclesiastical pretensions. The authority of the Civil Constitution of the Clergy was thus nil, and the civil oath of the clergy an "act of the most atrocious despotism."

The constitutional catechisms, in contrast, cited past cases of civil intervention in church matters, apostolic precedents of poverty, elections of bishops, and rights of the laity to speak out on matters of faith. . . . Papal bulls on these matters, it insisted, were to be ignored. The Catholic authors, once confident in combat with the philosophes, became strident, having been put on the defensive and legally excluded, whereas the constitutional catechist, with the backing of the government, could adopt a more tolerant tone. . . .

Apprehensions of a coming conflict soon became apparent to both constitutional and refractory clergy. In a pastoral instruction for Lent, the constitutional bishop Luc-François Lalande spoke of the specter of civil war and urged the refractory clergy, who were being legally repressed and thus emigrating in great numbers, to return to "the heart of their motherland." He prayed that God would "snuff out all the hatreds and all the divisions which trouble and tear apart our cities and countryside; that He fill our hearts with this spirit of union and fraternity which alone can assure public happiness. . . . The greatest crime is to light up the flame of civil war and to wish to bathe oneself in one's brother's blood." . . .

For the sake of peace, Louis XVI had approved the Civil Constitution of the Clergy on 24 August 1790 and had implored the pope to do likewise. But the king heartily disapproved of the Civil Constitution in principle and declined to approve the ecclesiastical oath of 27 November 1790 until the end of that December, when he temporized, in the hope that revolutionary enthusiasms would abate.

Pope Pius VI (1775–99), after months of delay, took the opposite course. On 10 March and 13 April, he published two briefs that condemned the Civil Constitution of the Clergy and various principles contained in the Declaration of the Rights of Man and the Citizen. These briefs reveal a vision of man and society diametrically opposed to that of the Revolution and are valuable in explaining some of the issues of the civil-religious war that broke out in France and Europe within a year. . . .

Some clerics retracted their oath, and the king turned more decisively against the Civil Constitution, refusing to sanction a law deporting refractory priests, but the schism continued to worsen. The competition between constitutional and refractory clergy contributed to the secularization of the state, as had granting toleration to Protestants and Jews. Each clergy held separate registers of births, marriages, and deaths and contested the legitimacy of any other. . . . The Revolution effectively created "two Frances." The civil state of marriage, moreover, was not indissoluble. This same law introduced divorce by mutual consent.

Even before the publication of the papal briefs, the National Assembly made a decision that symbolized France's secularization. On 4 April 1791, two days after Mirabeau's death, the assembly approved a proposal that the Church of Sainte-Geneviève, which Louis XV had commissioned in gratitude to the patron saint of Paris, be converted into a pantheon to honor great men of the patrie [fatherland]. The marquis de Pastoret, who initiated the act of secularization, explained that "the temple of religion should become the temple of the *patrie;* the tomb of a great man should become the altar of liberty." On 11 July, in an elaborate ceremony attended by some 200,000 people, the remains of an implacable enemy of Christianity were transferred to the former church. Voltaire, who had been denied a Christian burial in 1778, came to repose in the Panthéon, the erstwhile temple of Sainte-Geneviève, the fifth-century nun whose remains would soon be scattered in the Seine.

# Reinventing Education for a Democratic Citizenry

Crane Brinton

The leaders of the Revolution sought to reorganize and improve France's educational system to serve their new, classless, more democratic society. According to the late, highly respected Harvard University scholar Crane Brinton, these men envisioned indoctrinating the young with revolutionary political views to create new generations familiar with and loyal to the Revolution's ideals. Despite this overzealous, somewhat limiting approach, Brinton points out, the new system made significant strides in higher education, laying the groundwork for the free, secular, universal, and compulsory public schools now common throughout Western society.

The Revolution hardly achieved what more unexcited democracies have failed to achieve, a distinction in practice between education and propaganda. In spite of the eloquence of their master Rousseau, the Jacobins were quite unwilling to allow the child to find his own way through trial and error. Their notion of education was pretty close to pure indoctrination. When the Convention decreed that free and compulsory education was the concern of the state, it passed on to local administrations the task of procuring suitable teachers for the new elementary schools. The administrations in turn consulted the "people" assembled in the Jacobin clubs. Many of the resulting debates have survived in the papers of these clubs. Almost universally, the first question as to a proposed candidate for a teaching position was

Excerpted from pages 151–54 of *A Decade of Revolution, 1789–1799*, by Crane Brinton. Copyright 1934 by Harper & Row, Publishers, Inc. Copyright renewed 1961 by Crane Brinton. Reprinted by permission of HarperCollins Publishers, Inc.

directed towards his political orthodoxy and—what was much the same—his virtue. The opinion was commonly expressed that a good man could teach well even though he were ignorant. Only occasionally does a club admit that it "ought not to pass lightly over the question of talents."

## "Give Us a Generation"

The Revolution had to the full the modern passion for education, the modern faith that in education lies an earthly salvation. Most modern beliefs centering on education originated in the eighteenth century, and were first raised to the power of stereotypes by the French Revolution. Almost rivaling Danton's "de l'audace, encore de l'audace, toujours de l'audace" ["audacity, more audacity, always audacity," which he claimed would allow the people to save France] in the hearts of his countrymen is his assertion that "after bread, the first need of the people is education." To any of its critics, the Revolution could always reply: "Our difficulties arise from the fact that we are forced to deal with men and women brought up with bad habits, superstitious, ignorant, and too old to learn better; give us a generation, and we will bring up the young as citizens of a democracy should be brought up, and all will be well." The argument has since been repeated.

The old bad education of monarchical France was destroyed as completely as possible. Education in old France had had all the diversity of the old régime. Dame schools and charity schools brought simple literacy, at least, within reach of some of the lower classes. Secondary education was wholly in the hands of the church, and was limited to nobility and bourgeoisie. The curriculum was strictly classical, and pedagogical methods had not yet been seriously affected by the work of Rousseau. Indeed, the great intellectual effort of the Age of Enlightenment lay almost wholly outside teaching circles, and penetrated rather late into the formal academic world. By its confiscation of the property of the clergy and by its dissolution of monastic orders, the Constituent Assembly undermined the best part of primary and secondary education. The universities, headed by the ancient University of Paris, had undergone in the eighteenth century a decline similar to that of the great English universities in that same century, and their suppression by the Revolution was probably no great loss. None of the revolutionary assemblies succeeded in erecting a complete system of national education to replace the unsystematic institutions destroyed by the Revolution; none succeeded even in putting primary education on a broader quantitative basis than it had had during the old régime. Indeed, with the abolition of the teaching orders, the general economic crisis, the conservatism and timidity of the maiden ladies who used to run small private schools, it was probably harder to get a child taught his ABC's in 1793–1795 than it had been in 1788. Some practical improvement was made under the Directory, and it is but fair to add that the Convention itself laid down a platform that has subsequently been realized in most modern nations: free and compulsory primary education, and a system of state schools wholly separated from any organized Christian sect.

## Strides Made in Higher Education

In secondary and in higher education the revolution has a more definite achievement. In place of the *collèges*, the clerically controlled secondary schools of the old régime, the Convention set up in each department an *école centrale* [central school]. These schools developed very successfully until they were abolished by the bureaucratic Napoleon. Their curriculum gave full attention to the sciences and mathematics, and to the so-called social sciences, as well as to the older philosophical and rhetorical subjects. They had adequate libraries and laboratories. Their students were given considerable freedom of choice as to subjects studied, and what is more astonishing, administrative work was kept at a minimum, and done by the teaching staff itself without political supervision. The cities which possessed these schools were very proud of them, and contemporary opinion is almost universal in their praise.

In the field of higher education the Revolution established special schools which were to have a distinguished career in the next century. The "École des travaux publics" [school of public works] became the "École polytechnique" of today,

## Condorcet's Report on Education

*One of the most important acts of the Legislative Assembly, which first convened in October 1791, was the appointment of a committee to reorganize the system of education. The following are excerpts from the committee's general report, presented to the Assembly on April 20, 1792, by Marie-Jean, marquis de Condorcet (1743–1794), a well-known mathematician, philosopher, and member of the Academy of Science. The main thrust of the report was that education is the basis of human progress and that the state must use the schools to shape the views of future generations for the betterment of both France and a larger humanity.*

Gentlemen,

To offer all individuals of the human race the means of providing for their needs, of assuring their well-being, of knowing and exercising their rights, of understanding and performing their duties;

To assure each of them the facility of perfecting his skill, of rendering himself capable of the social functions to which he has a right to be summoned, of developing to the fullest extent the talents with which Nature has endowed him; and thereby to establish among citizens an actual equality, and to effect the realization of the political equality recognized by law:

Such must be the primary aim of national education; and from this point of view it is a task of probity [honest endeavor] for the government. . . .

Thus, education must be universal, that is to say, it must extend to all citizens. It must be shared as equally as the necessary limitations of expense, the distribution of population, and the greater or lesser amount of time that children may devote to it permit. It must, in its several degrees, comprise the entire system of human knowledge, and assure to men of all ages the facility of preserving their knowledge or of acquiring new knowledge.

John H. Stewart, ed., *A Documentary Survey of the French Revolution.* New York: Macmillan, 1951, pp. 347, 349, 361, 369–70.

one of the best technical schools in the world. The "École normale" of 1795 was hardly more than a series of lectures given by the greatest scholars and scientists of France to the more ambitious teachers of the new republic, but it contained the germ of the "École normale supérieure" [teachers' college] which was—surprising as the fact will seem to an American—one of the important forces in the making of modern France. Three medical schools were founded—at Montpellier, at Strasbourg, and at Paris—which, incorporated in the higher education of the empire, became productive centers of medical research.

The true Jacobin, however, was always more interested in the culture of the heart than in the culture of the head. With all his devotion to the Enlightenment, he never trusted the free human intellect. Mere thinking never kept a man straight. Virtue must be sought in the communion of man with man. The republic has a perpetual job of adult education far more important than the ABC's. Its citizens must feel the mystic identity of the general will. The Terror was constantly preoccupied with a suitable cult, a suitable ritual, for the Republic of Virtue.

# The Role of Women in the Revolution

Olwen Hufton

Although Frenchwomen did not enjoy the same political rights as men despite the Revolution's liberal declaration of rights and national constitution, both of which stressed equality, they played an important, influential role throughout the early years of the Revolution. Olwen Hufton, a professor of modern history at England's University of Harvard and an authority on women during the Revolution, offers this very informative overview. He begins with an account of Parisian women asserting themselves in bread riots and in marching to Versailles to make demands of the king, and goes on to describe how many *sans-culotte* wives aided the Revolution by supporting their politically active husbands; Hufton also pays close attention to moderate and radical feminist groups who loudly, but in the end unsuccessfully, tried to gain a political voice equal to that of men.

For the constitution makers of the Constituent Assembly the question of who should exercise political power as full citizens was a moot point. Excluded from voting even in primary elections were three kinds of people: those who did not pay tax equivalent to the income from three days labour; servants deemed incapable, because of the nature of their occupation, of objective behaviour; and women. The first two exclusions were hotly debated. Indeed, Robespierre virtually established his political reputation on his attack on the limitations of the male franchise. . . . The third exclusion

Reprinted from Olwen Hufton, "Voilà la Citoyenne," *History Today*, May 1989, by permission of *History Today*.

went unquestioned. A woman, whose full rational powers were scarcely conceded by the Enlightenment, was not deemed a political animal but one dependent upon the decisions of husband or father with whom she must agree. . . .

Yet the chronicle of Revolution is markedly different. A conspicuous characteristic of events between 1790 and 1796 is the often dramatic intervention of women. Beginning with the march to Versailles in 1789 and culminating in the riots of *germinal* and *prairial* in the year III which marked the end of the popular revolution, we see women heavily involved in actions of political moment and consequence which shaped the course of national history. Furthermore, it is in the closing decades of the eighteenth century, lent sharpness by the revolutionary situation, that the origins of modern feminism are traditionally located. We discern the first coherent attempts to claim for women, civil, legal, social and in some instances political, parity with men.

Women, however, were far from speaking in a single voice. In the course of the Revolution they were to demonstrate an infinite variety of responses to change which reflected local conditions or individual convictions ranging from hearty endorsement to overt hostility to the measures from the capital. The real 'revolutionary' woman, the *maîtresse ès Révolution* [mistress of the Revolution], was without any doubt the working woman of the Paris *quartiers:* the counter-revolutionary was the peasant woman who resented the intrusion of the Revolution in her life and the hardships imposed. Between these two extremes existed an entire range of attitudes, changing over time. . . .

## Working Women Protect Their Interests

The working women of Paris emerged first and foremost as intrepid defenders of the bread-basket in October 1789. The great march to Versailles is part of a long tradition of women's participation in the bread riot. The people of Paris were consumers not producers of bread. As wage earners and small artisans, price rises in the basic foodstuff spelled intolerable hardship to them. Women were purchasers of and negotiators for bread in the market place. Not only were they sensitive to prices, but they had a special role to play in defence of the consumer-interests of the family. They were the protagonists of that ancient 'moral economy' in which a just price, one which put a plentiful bread supply within the reach of every wage earner, was the concern. As women, however, they were also legatees of an old western European tradition of direct female action in the market place to protect their interests as purchasers. This tradition, whose assumptions were being questioned in eighteenth-century England, was still very much alive in France and the Netherlands. Women believed themselves invested with specific (and never defined) powers to riot without incurring legal action if certain rules were respected. Such rules included respect for property, consciousness of producer or distributor malpractice in forcing up commodity prices, and a knowledge that a disturbance could not be protracted. . . . The more fundamental purpose was to demonstrate to those in authority, which in the context of 1789 could only mean the king, that his people, innocent families, were suffering. . . .

When, in the aftermath of the fall of the Bastille, prices did not fall and the king and the politicians at Versailles seemed locked in stalemate, a step was taken to impress on the king the people's plight. The working women of the Paris *quartiers* did what their great-great grandmothers had done in the terrible winter of 1708–1709. They went to Versailles to reach the king directly and explain to him their suffering. Their action in one sense had no originality; the technique was time-honoured. On the other hand, this time the twinning of the bread and political issues had, in the context of revolution, a new consequence; a demand for plentiful bread at a reasonable price was accompanied by a cry to bring the king and his family back to Paris. The chief-baker must know what was going on. He must be made to leave the artificiality of the court. Here, the movement assumed originality. A demonstration of which women, to the profound disbelief of subsequent nineteenth-century British historians, were the architects and in which they predominated, brought the king, followed by the politicians, back into the capital. A protest traditional enough in form had been invested with immense political consequence. The degree to which the crowd at Versailles was manipulated to demand the king's return to Paris remains an area of debate but that the October Days were women's days was not disputed territory in the context of Revolution. They were also an immense consciousness-raising exercise for both the women of the masses and for those who believed in a greater civic and political role for women.

## Assuming a More Active Role

The two need at this stage to be somewhat differentiated. The working women of Paris, laundresses, garment-workers, spinners, shopkeepers were not passive women locked in a private sphere. They learned in the course of 1789 that direct action could bring about change, but this did not necessarily link itself to notions of civic or political parity with men. Citizenship as understood by the Constituent Assembly was, in any case, based upon a property or income qualification which excluded well over a third of the adult male population, and debates on who should hold political power were only beginning. Nonetheless, amongst those who went to Versailles or who brooded upon the lesson of the October Days were a few, perhaps no more at this stage than a handful, prepared to embark upon a more ambitious political programme demanding full citizenship rights for some or all women. Amongst them was Olympe de Gouges who over the next two years wrote the *Déclaration des droits de la femme et de la citoyenne* [*Declaration of the Rights of Woman and Citizen*].

Notions that women could and should assume an active role as architects of a new social order were in the air. Women's clubs mushroomed all over France in the 1790s although they were mostly directed towards philanthropy [charity work] or were of middle-class women prepared to assume responsibility for explaining measures such as the Civil Constitution of the Clergy to a bewildered populace. . . .

In the course of 1790–92, the women of the Paris sections developed, as did their husbands, an awareness of themselves as architects of a revolution which must, because it existed with their connivance, be made to represent their interests. . . .

## The Good *Sans-Culotte*'s Wife

By 1792 there had evolved something which could be labelled a 'revolutionary mentality'. . . . Drawing on the rhetoric of the clubs, sectionial politics and the popular press, not least by Hébert's influential *Père Dûchesne* [a popular radical newspaper], [there emerged] a couple, the good *sans-culotte* and his wife. A *sans-culotte* had to be married, because a bachelor could not fully comprehend the problems of a family man. Our good *sans-culotte* and his wife believed that Revolution had taken place with their help to remedy popular grievances, high prices, and government corruption. Both believed implicitly in the corruption of king and ministers. . . . Both were for the war at the outset in defence of their revolution. They sent their sons to the front. They made personal monetary sacrifices. But their bitterness and anxiety grew with news of military disaster, traitorous generals, the approach of the Prussians towards Paris . . . all of which seemed a betrayal of their interests, and they were mobilised into national acts of revenge like the prison massacres and ultimately, and more pertinently, to the overthrow of the constitution and the elimination of the Girondins.

Can one distinguish between the good *sans-culotte* and his wife? Certainly the pages of Hébert are full of material which allows the same type of caricature . . . made for Pierre Manuel, Hébert's model *sans-culotte*, to be drawn for his wife. . . .

Pierre Manuel's wife was first and foremost a wife and a mother of at least three children of whom one was at the front and the others needing her honest direction in sound revolutionary principles. She was a housewife of remorseless thrift and ingenuity. Words are put into her mouth like the following:

> I need to know how to manage, how could I not when I have a husband who drinks for six and eats for four and a regiment of children with ever open mouths? . . .

She spent most of her time in the home, preparing meals, or at the market and in the wash-place. She talked with other women on her staircase, in the streets, and whilst washing linen. . . . She was the eyes and ears of Pierre Manuel, informing him of the realities of the situation, what was going on in the streets, since he was more than occupied working to support his family. Her priorities are plain. First, rearing her children. . . .

A woman's political career is first of all raising citizens.

But if she had the time (and since she was Pierre Manuel's helpmate, she must also work, if in a more casual capacity), she should attend executions to ensure that the Terror was working properly. Clean and chaste, a good plain cook with an ugly face and a total indifference to finery, she is shown to lack all artifice but to have a vision of a future when treachery would be eliminated and everyone would be as honest as she was. . . .

More than anything else she was a proud woman, proud of her family, her housekeeping, and her Revolution.

## Female Ferocity

To what extent was caricature based upon reality? Police files endorse an intense commitment of women to eliminating counter-revolution, denouncing *propos inciviques* (utterances critical of the Revolution), hoarders, speculators, aristocrats.

The spectacle of women before the guillotine with blood splashing the stockings they are knitting for the soldiers at the front is both legendary and founded in fact. Politicians quailed before what they identified as 'female ferocity' which they interpreted as unfeminine since it failed to conform to their notions of what was fitting for their wives and daughters. Yet it represented what working women interpreted as a judgement on those who would undermine the Revolution. They did not hesitate to confront officialdom on practical issues they deemed important, such as news of their sons at the front. For them, politicians were meant to be available and sensitive to the public. The explicit and intense commitment of women to Marat, which raised him after his death to the category of martyr, stems from his readiness to be available to their complaints and his frank admiration for their single-mindedness. . . .

## Moderate Feminists

We should perhaps be careful not to overstress the uniformity of attitudes and ideas within these groups. Olympe de Gouges, for example, who believed in the civic parity of women, was committed to the Girondin faction which leaves little doubt that she was far from thinking that *all* women had the right to representation. Indeed she was very afraid of the women of the masses. When club life developed rapidly in 1790–92, some women (again one can only name a handful) used this means to advance claims for the natural rights of women. Etta Palm d'Aelders for example used the *Cercle Social* [*Social Circle*, a club that lobbied for women's rights] . . . to chastise the politicians for the Revolution's failure to acknowledge women's rights to social and civic parity and to encourage women in a civic and philanthropic role. With the advent of war, Pauline Léon presented to the Legislative a petition signed by 319 women requesting to form a *garde nationale feminine* of armed women to defend Paris. Twenty days later Théroigne de Méricourt called for the creation of legions of amazons to defend the Revolution.

Yet the clubs scarcely troubled the surface of Parisian political life. . . . Such indications as we have, suggest a low attendance rate and we must ask why? A chasm lay between the very bourgeois programmes of these clubs and the aspirations of the majority of Parisian women. The clubs were sensitive to poverty, but they never talked about the price of bread. . . . An association by the women of the clubs with the Girondins ensured that the bulk of Parisian working women, in so far as they were aware of their existence, were actually hostile to them. . . .

These [more moderate, middle-class] women were perceived by fellow women to have nothing to offer to the popular cause.

## More Women

The same was not necessarily true of the *Société républicaine révolutionnaire* [*Revolutionary Republican Society*], founded in

May 1793. The women involved declared their founding principle to be to deliberation and action to frustrate the plans of the enemies of the Republic. . . .

Two days later the same women read an address to the Jacobins demanding measures to disarm all suspects, to form legions of armed amazons and denouncing women who eschewed an active role in Revolution. The audience was not receptive to the notion of armed women but the president preserved harmony by an evasive if genial response. The new women's club also declared an open war on hoarders and inflation. Here was the only issue perhaps capable of drawing into a club the working women in Paris. Yet we know nothing of how many joined its sessions. One estimate is as low as sixty-seven, another 100, the women claimed the support of thousands and the Jacobins certainly believed their programme capable of rallying women on a massive scale. Its deliberations have been lost. It seems from the signatures to petitions to have largely been composed of small tradeswomen who could at least sign their names. The leaders were very competent militants prepared to use the right of petitioning, to organise mass demonstrations and to make a nuisance of themselves to further their ends. The energy of the activists was striking: endorsing petitions . . . for an acceleration of the Terror and the trial of the Girondins; attempting to enter the Convention without tickets to press the Girondin leaders; and demanding the right to participate in the *Comité Révolutionnaire* [committee having the power to arrest suspected enemies of the Revolution]. They could rightly feel they played a positive role in the fall of the Girondins in June by the effective use of political weapons.

## Radical Women Silenced by the Jacobins

The harmonious relationship between the club and the Jacobins did not live long after the fall of the Girondins. The women were not passive supporters of any faction and they were explicitly critical of the Jacobins' reluctance to move to a policy of controlled prices. In July 1793 Claire Lacombe charged the politicians with calculated delaying over the arrest of suspects and with not having the people's interests at heart. Pauline Léon followed with a proposal to petition the Convention for new elections, given the dilatoriness of the existing deputies in accelerating the Terror and the war on hoarders. . . .

By October 30th, 1793 . . . the Jacobin politicians had . . . closed all the women's clubs and had excluded women from all other political societies. Why did they do this? Why were they apparently afraid of the actions of the 170 women?

The answer seems to lie in the politicians' fear of the women's potential to rouse a broader populace and from the continued embarrassment of their pressure through petitioning and occupation of the Convention for an acceleration of the Terror. Two factors stand out in the engineering of their fall. First they were denounced by a petition from the . . . market women *against* price fixing. . . . In short, women were denounced by women. Second, the rhetoric of denunciation was totally inconsistent: some politicians charged the *clubistes* with *indulgence* (over-leniency to traitors), others with irrational ferocity. Were the denouncers the tools of the politicians? The records are silent. What is apparent, however, is the failure of the club to secure a massive female demonstration on its behalf. . . .

When [Pierre] Chaumette [an extreme radical revolutionary] pronounced the closure of the women's clubs he reminded *sans-culotte* women that they should leave politics to their husbands and tend to their families whilst their husbands went to their club. [André] Amar in the Convention gave voice to the masculine majority when he said 'a woman's honour confines her to the private sphere and precludes her from a struggle with men'. . . .

[By late 1794,] as a revolutionary force, the women of Paris were exhausted. The leaders of the clubs were dead, in prison or had fled. . . . Prices soared, paper currencies had no value and the black market was triumphant. The day of the urban revolutionary woman was over: that of the counter-revolutionary peasant woman was dawning.

# Chapter 4

# The French Revolution's Impact and Legacy

Turning|Points
IN WORLD HISTORY

# How the Revolution Affected the French People

William Doyle

The French Revolution affected the French people in both negative and positive ways, argues the distinguished scholar William Doyle, chairman of the School of History at the University of Bristol. On the negative side, the evolution of revolutionary government ended with dictatorship and even more governmental intrusion in people's personal lives than had existed under the monarchy. Yet the Revolution benefited many groups in the long run, Doyle explains, among them property owners, middle-class professionals, Protestants, Jews, soldiers, and slaves. Revolutionary leaders granted the latter freedom in Saint-Domingue, the French-controlled Caribbean island that became the independent nation of Haiti in 1804.

Was . . . the Revolution worth it in material terms? For most ordinary French subjects turned by it into citizens, it cannot have been. It had made their lives infinitely more precarious, when they had expected the reverse. It had bidden fair to destroy the religious, cultural, and moral underpinnings of the communities in which they lived. The *cahiers* of 1789 make overwhelmingly clear that most French people wanted less state interference in their lives, yet it brought far more, and fiercer. Government by terror scarcely outlasted the Year II, but nothing like it had ever occurred before. When it ebbed, the power of the State remained, permanently augmented and disposing of coercive powers not dreamed of by the old monarchy. It was no wonder therefore, that the most persistent and massive resistance that the Revolution encountered

Reprinted from William Doyle, *The Oxford History of the French Revolution*, © William Doyle, 1989, by permission of Oxford University Press.

came not from the former so-called 'privileged orders' but from ordinary people who simply wanted to call a halt. In alienating so many of their fellow citizens, the revolutionaries furnished counter-revolutionaries with constant hope and encouragement. But most popular resistance was anti- rather than counter-revolutionary. Though they might mouth slogans about restoring Church and king, all most anti-revolutionaries wanted was stability and autonomy after years of upheaval and intrusion by outsiders. Their resistance, however, only too often pushed France's new authorities to further extremes of repression, gouging existing wounds yet wider and deeper.

Popular rejection of what the Revolution had become . . . was endemic throughout the south, where the Revolution was perceived as designed to benefit rich Protestants; and broke out periodically in rioting on local issues in many other areas. The statistics of emigration and terror are also suggestive. Almost 32,000, a third of all registered *émigrés*, were peasants or workers turning their backs on the land of liberty. Of the official victims of the Terror, 8,350, or almost 60 per cent, were from the same groups, dying for their resistance. Deserters or draft-dodgers, tellingly defined as 'insubordinate' (*insoumis*), were another gauge. In 1789 drawing for the militia, one of the most hated institutions of the old order, had been abolished. By 1793 it was back, and in 1798 conscription assumed a far more systematic character. Evasion of military service was universally agreed to be a major ingredient in the rural crime wave which marked the directorial period. 'Many deserters are lurking about the woods', wrote an English traveller through Chantilly in 1796, 'and there are continual robberies and murders. We have not travelled half an hour in the dark.' Banditti, he called them later on: bandits—a category social scientists have learned to recognize as a classic form of protest against an established order. . . .

## Property Owners and the Professions

Yet some groups undoubtedly gained. In any list of them, pride of place must go to the owners of land. Freed in August 1789 from the burdens of feudalism and the tithe, they were able to proclaim property as the supreme social and political commodity. The Civil Code, when it was completed, consolidated and clarified their rights, and the means of transmitting them. Successive constitutions, in one way or another, made the effective exercise of political rights dependent in turn on property. Property would define the class of Notables who ruled France, as electors, from the Consulate down to the late nineteenth century. The social profile of property owners was little altered by the Revolution. The amount of land held by the nobility inevitably fell, although in the 1800s they still dominated the ranks of the largest and richest proprietors. At the other end of the scale the sale of national lands, especially in the mid-1790s when they had been marketed in small lots, had produced an increase in the number of petty peasant owners, though their overall share scarcely rose. The great gainers from the redistribution of church and noble property were the bourgeoisie. More than anything else, their fears about the security of their gains finally pushed the Revolution into the hands of a dictator [Napoleon] who imposed stability and offered all property owners unconditional recognition of their title. By the time he fell, their grip on their gains was beyond challenge, and the restored Bourbons, though they returned émigré lands still unsold and organized a fund to compensate those whose property had gone, never seriously thought of undoing the land settlement bequeathed by the Revolution.

The bourgeoisie also gained by the Revolution, in the end, as the group from which the professions were recruited. The men of 1789 had proclaimed careers open to the talents, believing that neither birth nor wealth should give privileged access to any employment. At first the implementation of this principle looked like developing into a disaster for the professions. . . . The Revolution was early hostile to professional associations in general, interpreting their commitment to maintaining standards as a hangover from the now abandoned world of corporatism and privilege. 'This was one of the first abuses of freedom', recalled a distinguished lawyer, 'that the right was left to anyone, without scrutiny, or any apprenticeship, to practise the liberal professions.' Medicine, the bar, and the law in general were thrown open to the market, with minimal qualifications required from practitioners. Most of the former validating bodies, like universities, were abolished in any case. Revolutionary France was therefore a happy hunting ground for quacks and charlatans of every sort—most of them, to be sure, members of the bourgeoisie too. Not until Napoleonic times did the State take the situation in hand and reintroduce a rigorous system of licensing to restore professional standards. The solution was more bureaucratic than before 1789—but then so was France. . . .

## Soldiers

Another group who did well out of the Revolution were soldiers. In no sphere were careers thrown more open to the talents, as the most successful careerist of them all was always ready to testify. Although military careers continued to attract high numbers of nobles still throughout the nineteenth century, the aristocratic monopoly of the officer corps had gone for ever. Proclaimed in 1789, equal opportunity in the army became a reality far more suddenly than could have been naturally expected when discipline collapsed and a large proportion of officers emigrated over the next two years. By 1793, accordingly, 70 per cent of officers in service had risen from the ranks. Even the officer-entry nobles who were left had their promotional chances improved by the departure of so many of their fellows. And for more than two decades after this, the vastly expanded army, first of the Great Nation, then of the Napoleonic Empire, would offer glory and good prospects to those who joined it and stayed with the colours. It was, of course, dangerous. By 1802 400,000 French men had fallen in battle, and another million, perhaps, would follow them before night fell on the field of Waterloo [site of Napoleon's final defeat]. The thousands of draft-dodgers and deserters who evaded each call-up showed clearly enough that the army's appeal was far from universal. Yet there was no mistaking the enthusiasm, commitment, and revolutionary arrogance of the Republic's armies. From the start soldiers were among the most fervent

146 The French Revolution

and extreme revolutionaries, scorning officers who still behaved like aristocrats, lynching generals suspected of treachery, cheering on dechristianization, and vigorously imposing the bracing discipline of liberty on defeated enemies. By 1795 and 1796, the opportunities for looting and plunder were limitless, and those lucky enough to be in the army of Italy had the unique privilege of being paid in coin. By 1797 the armies saw themselves in the former sansculotte mantle as guardians of the Revolution's purity, standing ready to intervene in domestic politics under any successful general who would mouth slogans about saving the Republic from feckless babblers. When eventually the luckiest of such generals took power, military style was imposed on the State. . . .

## Protestants and Jews

Landowners, the bourgeoisie, bureaucrats, soldiers—all these groups did well out of the Revolution, taking advantage of the circumstances it had brought about. Certain others benefited from deliberate and conscious acts of emancipation. Most prominent among them were the Protestants. Although the monarchy had been moving towards a more tolerant attitude with its grant of civil status in 1787, French Protestants welcomed the Revolution almost unanimously as their true benefactor, proclaiming as it did freedom of thought and worship and full equality of civil rights between all French citizens. They were quick to lay claim to these rights, too—with inflammatory results in the cities of the south where old Catholic élites lost power as a result. Their triumph there merely confirmed their age-old reputation in Catholic eyes as subversives and troublemakers. Their early commitment did not save them in 1793 from the ravages of terror and dechristianization. . . . In the cities churches opened only a couple of years earlier (often in premises formerly the property of the Catholic Church) were closed or transformed into temples of reason. . . . Yet the annexation of Geneva in 1798 added the most famous Calvinist centre of all to French territory, and consular realism refused to countenance any return to Catholic legal dominance. In fact, under Bonaparte, the Protestant churches were established on a parallel basis to the Catholic, with salaried pastors. . . . [By 1815,] there was no going back on the rights and status accorded to Protestants at the start of the Revolution, and confirmed by Bonaparte when he ended it.

The Revolution also brought emancipation to France's 39,000 Jews. Here again there had been signs of change before 1789. The name of Grégoire first came to public notice when in 1784 he won the Academy of Metz's essay competition on the theme of how the lot of Jews could be improved. In the same year a number of legal disadvantages borne by the Jews of Alsace were lifted, and when the Revolution began the government was planning further concessions in what it, and Jewish leaders too, regarded as a natural corollary to the moves in favour of Protestants. Yet the National Assembly proved in much less of a hurry to grant Jews the full rights of French citizens. When the issue was debated (which it was not until the last days of 1789) it became clear that many did not regard them as French at all. . . . Not until . . . 27 September 1791 were they admitted to full citizenship, against the vocal opposition of the Alsatian future Director, Reubell. Strictly speaking, dechristianization could not be applied to Jews; but the practice of their religion was still persecuted in 1793 and 1794 by the Montagnard zealots of Alsace, who remembered that Jewish fanaticism and superstition were as much condemned by Voltaire and other prophets of progress as by undiminished popular prejudice. Prejudice remained when terror ended. . . . Not, however, until 1805 did the government intervene again in Jewish affairs, and then Napoleon's aim was to consolidate their position as citizens, if only by imposing closer state control on their activities. There was to be no return to the marginal status of before the 1780s—much to the disgust of the anti-Semites who continued to be found throughout French society.

## The Beginning of the End of Slavery

Finally, reluctantly and belatedly, the Revolution also abolished slavery. In contrast to the case of Protestants and Jews, there was little expectation of change in this sphere before

1789. Although most of the *philosophes* had condemned slavery and the trade which sustained it, the first French abolition society, the Amis des Noirs, was not founded by Brissot until 1788. Only a handful of *cahiers* mentioned the issue, and the defenders of slavery were well organized and funded by the wealth of the colonial trade. They dominated the colonial committee of the National Assembly. But when the Assembly voted, in July 1789, to admit unconvoked deputies from Saint-Domingue [the Caribbean island originally called Hispaniola and now made up of the nations of Haiti and the Dominican Republic] did so only after a long and bitter debate about whom they represented. It had raised the question of the political rights of the numerous and increasingly well-organized free coloured population, not to mention the black slaves. And whereas, its decision made, the Assembly passed on to pressing metropolitan business, the impact on the colony itself was volcanic. Struggles for political control now began there between whites and free coloureds, culminating in an uprising of the latter in October 1790 which the whites put down with great brutality. . . . News of these clashes provoked a new debate in Paris, and in May 1791 the Assembly, at the urging of deputies like Grégoire and Robespierre, granted civil rights to coloureds born of two free parents. It was the Revolution's first gesture towards racial equality; but before news of it could reach Saint-Domingue, the slaves, stirred up by the ferocity of the political conflicts around them, had risen in the great rebellion of August 1791. It was the progress of this uprising that forced the pace on racial issues. In April 1791 the Legislative, of which Brissot was the most prominent member, granted full rights to all free coloureds regardless of parentage. But when commissioners sent out to enforce the new law arrived in the colony, they found the situation so envenomed that it made little impact. Within months of their arrival, France was at war with Great Britain, and communications with home perilous. Willy-nilly the commissioners were forced to use their own initiative in responding to a complex and shifting situation. Thus . . . by the beginning of February 1793 Commissioner Sonthonax was beginning to denounce 'aristocrats of the skin'. The latter responded by trying to drive the commissioners from the colony by force. Only nonwhites defended Sonthonax, and in recognition of this in June 1793 he offered freedom to all blacks who would fight for the Republic. 'It is', he declared, 'with the natives of the country, that is, the Africans, that we will save Saint-Domingue for France.' Two months later, as Spaniards from the other part of the island invaded the troubled colony, he took the final step. On 29 August, slavery itself was abolished in the northern province. In October general freedom was proclaimed for all Saint-Domingue. None of this had been authorized by the Convention. . . . But when news of the emancipation arrived in Paris in January 1794 the Convention greeted it with enthusiasm, if only because, like Sonthonax, the deputies saw it as a way to defeat the Republic's British and Spanish enemies in the Caribbean. On 4 February, accordingly, the Convention framed its own decree: Negro slavery was abolished in all French colonies, and all men living there were citizens with full rights.

The effect was dramatic. As soon as the news arrived in the colony, late in April, black rebel leaders began to rally to the Republic. The free black Toussaint L'Ouverture, who had joined the Spanish invaders, switched sides. The Spaniards were driven out by black forces, who proceeded to massacre whites who had welcomed the invaders. Under the peace Of 1795 Spain ceded all of Hispaniola to France. . . . Slavery lasted . . . in French colonies down to 1848. But it was never re-established in Saint-Domingue, which proclaimed itself, on 1 January 1804, the Republic of Haiti. . . .

French control over the former richest colony in the world was never regained. Haiti was thus the only truly independent state to come into being as a result of the French Revolution.

# The Revolution's Influence on Later World Revolutions

Jacques Solé

This essay is excerpted from the intriguing book *Questions of the French Revolution: A Historical Overview*, published in 1989 to coincide with the Revolution's globally observed bicentennial. The author, French scholar Jacques Solé, a professor at the University of Social Sciences at Grenoble, identifies influences of the 1789 French political and social upheavals in later revolutionary and nationalistic activity in other countries, including Germany, Hungary, Italy, and Russia. Some revolutionary leaders, like Russia's Lenin, Solé points out, viewed the Terror orchestrated by Robespierre and his compatriots as necessary and useful and cited it to justify their own systematic use of political repression and violence.

For many, the story begun in 1789 has not ended. . . .

The French Revolution . . . gave rise to a new conception of world history. Political culture often was defined in relation to it, as the revolutions of the nineteenth and twentieth centuries demonstrate. They were so indebted to the event of 1789 because it invented the notion of revolution as a political change that was at once voluntary and total. Subsequent revolutions attempted to bring about similar transformations, making good use of the nationalistic ideology associated with a revolution that brought the fatherland to arms. This strange permutation of Enlightenment thought was not so much theorized as experienced anonymously by the entirety of a community [i.e., most people did not think about or relate directly to the French Revolution itself, but nevertheless used and benefited from its ideals and methods]. It is pointless to speculate whether the nationalism born of the victorious revolution really corresponded to the mentality of its leaders. It resulted above all from the events of the Revolution, from which its successors drew its lessons. The idea of a nation was new for France in 1789. With this impetus, it was to travel around the world, from a Europe trampled by its armies to Latin America, before spreading to the states born of decolonization. This creation of the political culture of the Revolution is, today, an essential element of France's prestige. The Revolution also produced the modern concepts of political terrorism and of a vanguard [popular, activist] party. It created conditions that spurred the development of conservative thought and the early stages in the elaboration of socialism. Attitudes toward history and social order could no longer be the same after 1799 as they had been before 1789. An ideological tidal wave, the French Revolution was, in this sense, the cradle of the modern world. Its long-range influence was to prove more important in this respect than in its immediate effects.

## The Common Property of European Intellectuals

It provided a decisive element to German philosophy in the early nineteenth century and was related, along with the Romantic tradition, to the rise of German nationalism, if only by provoking a backlash. In 1794 Hungarian Jacobins were executed, while their Polish counterparts, who had risen up against the Russian army, dreamed of an international revolutionary brotherhood of European democrats. During the first half of the nineteenth century the historiography of the French Revolution was the common property of all the intellectuals of the [European] Continent. From it they drew their plans for a repeat version, splitting into the camps of the liberals, who stopped with 1789, and the radicals, who did not reject the example of 1793 [i.e., the Terror]. The young Hungarian Jozsef Irinyi thus declared in 1846, "The Revolution begun in 1789 is not yet over." Two years later his compatriot Vasvari was to write that "the tree of liberty

must be watered with blood." . . . This admirer of Robespierre and his revolution, the world's new gospel and humanity's bible, was killed in a desperate fight to which he had
been pushed by moral imperatives springing from his adherence to the ideology born in 1789. These heroes were em-
ulated in 1956 during Budapest's revolt against a Stalinist
Soviet order [in 1956 the Hungarians tried unsuccessfully to
end Russian control of their country].

Of all the European countries, Italy was the most profoundly shaken by the French Revolution. Its mid-nineteenth-
century national unity movement owed much to this contact
after 1796. In many ways the culture of postrevolutionary
Italy no doubt grew out of the reformist tradition of the Enlightenment. But Italian democrats proclaimed their allegiance to the example of 1789 even more strongly. Among
them [Giuseppe] Mazzini was especially significant, as he
moved from justifying the Montagnard Terror in the early
1830s to opposing it, claiming that a repeat of 1793 would
be fatal to the interests of the republican party and the Italian revolution. Its leaders nevertheless constantly harked
back to the French Revolution. In 1870 its mythic aura likewise surrounded the nascent Italian socialist movement,
which was more appreciative than Mazzini in his later years
of the accomplishments of the Terror.

Even those authors least admiring of the French Revolution have noted the prestige it gained abroad when its legend
was elevated to sacred status. It has contributed much more
than memories of the *ancien régime* to the glory of France, for
it is considered a decisive phase in mankind's history, the
time and place where the various nations of the world began
to learn the lessons of freedom. This symbolism spread
through all of Latin America, where in the nineteenth century a number of republics were created on the French
model. And this movement was to be repeated in our own era
during the period of decolonization. To understand this one
needs only to have witnessed one of black Africa's countless
revolutions, which occurred, naturally, on the night of August 4: The power that was to be unseated was at the heart of
a Committee of Public Safety; the new leaders called for

people to be wary of enemies both within and without, to achieve victory or die for the fatherland, and to form, posthaste, committees for the defense of the revolution. . . .

## A Model for Communists?

The historical fortunes of Marxism [communism] also explain this shift. Its founders always granted key importance to the French Revolution, from the writings of the young [German socialist writer Karl] Marx to those of [Russian communist leader] Lenin, who created or inspired large numbers of governments that still trace their roots, in part, to their 1793 precursor. The events of 1789 do indeed constitute a source of Marxism since . . . this date served to pinpoint a period of world history in which feudalism and the *ancien régime* stood opposed to the rise of the bourgeoisie. This was made possible, according to Marx . . . only by the "community of revolutionary interests within the third estate." On a deeper level . . . the French Revolution provided the model for the Marxist conception of politics. . . . The founders of Marxism perceptively observed the dual character of the Revolution of 1789, which was at once the founding act of democracy and the first mirror of its contradictions. . . . Socialism was conceived primarily to resolve these, and thus to carry out the legacy of the French Revolution.

This was one of the ambitions of Lenin, who was always fascinated by the period of Jacobin predominance. Before turning late in life to the writings of Marat, he had accepted the comparison made in 1904 by his Menshevik adversaries between their struggle and the one that had split the Girondins and the Montagnards [the Mensheviks were moderate communists corresponding to the Girondin Jacobins, while the Bolsheviks were radicals corresponding to the Mountain faction of Jacobins]. This interpretation made the Bolsheviks, in turn, the conscious organizers of the revolution. Its leaders in early-twentieth-century Russia viewed their conflict in terms of the history of the Convention. Their concept of dictatorship was that of Robespierre and Saint-Just and their main goal was to imitate the great movement of 1789. In 1905 Lenin evoked with relish the prospect of a Terror. . . . Faced with an eventual counterrevolution, he openly proclaimed his adherence to Jacobin psychology and policy, which he viewed as authorizing the use of "revolutionary violence." In 1917 he identified his activities with the Jacobin example of "democratic revolution and defiance to the coalition of monarchs against the Republic." He praised the implacability of the Convention at its height and observed that its memory, loathed by the bourgeois and feared by the petty bourgeoisie, remained dear to the oppressed, for it bought them the hope of people's power. This concept of history stressed a hypothetical hegemony [dominance] of the masses during the year II. Pressed into the service of the communist cause, it long dominated a historiography that refused . . . to see the Mountain's dictatorship during the Terror as an enterprise that repressed the plebeian [common people's] movement. . . . [There are clear] echoes of Robespierre in the Lenin of 1917 who wanted to take away from "the capitalists their bread and all their boots," while hoping he would not be forced to send defenseless people to the guillotine. He too was soon obliged to justify his own Terror by the force of circumstances. The whole history of Bolshevism in power was written in the shadow of the Convention, and 1793 remained an essential point of reference. Lenin ended his career contemplating, like many of his eventual successors, the possibility of a Soviet Thermidor [moderate reaction to the ruling radicals]. This obsession brought Russia one step closer to eighteenth-century France. Lenin alluded several times to this in his public speeches and private notes. He was afraid that 1921 might be a repeat of 1794 [the year of the Thermidorian Reaction], but took comfort in the popular support he believed his government enjoyed.

## Its Greatness and Its Curse

Subsequent communist revolutions, from Peking to Havana, have not escaped this mythology, particularly since their debt to Leninism is immense and they view modern world history through its deforming prism. It was perhaps not wrong to place the French Revolution at the center of the comparative study of revolutions, since its image remains at the heart of the social and ideological movements of the nineteenth and twentieth centuries. One possible explanation . . . involves the concept of modernization, with revolution offering the advantage of political mobilization of the masses in the service of economic progress. Valid as it is for most of the revolutions of the twentieth century, this view does not seem to hold for that of 1789. For them, as for modern history as a whole, it served rather as a political educator. Its importance stems not only from its creation of the socioeconomic classes of the bourgeoisie and the proletariat, which did not exist before it, but also from the astonishing inventiveness with which, over the course of ten years, it tried out almost all the possible forms of modern government: constitutional monarchy, republic based on property qualifications, democratic republic, oligarchical republic, popular dictatorship, direct municipal democracy, military dictatorship, etc. An astounded world witnessed the rapid succession of these various notions of power on the French political scene. An incredibly fertile proving ground, the Revolution handed down to the future all its political games and all their rules after having created an enduring model for each.

The English-speaking countries have been almost the only ones untouched by this creativity and its influence, insofar as they had their own liberal tradition which proved, in practice, rather difficult to export. France dissociated itself likewise from them, at the time, by its rejection of the economic manifestations of modernity. Choosing political, rather than industrial revolution, it quickly elevated the state to sacred status, retaining its rural myths of a traditional society drawn from both its *ancien régime* heritage and the lessons of the republics of antiquity. What the world remembered of the French Revolution was its emphasis on class antagonisms and party conflict, and its taste for ideological radicalization and extreme solutions throughout the tumult of war at home and abroad. Since then, it has often been believed that nations and regimes were necessarily formed and dissolved after this pattern. The Revolution's greatness, and no doubt its curse as well, is that it invented modern politics.

# Modern Myths and Realities About the Revolution

Robert R. Palmer

As is the case in great historical events, over the centuries the French Revolution has generated a significant number of romanticized myths, which, blended with the facts, have come to affect the thinking of successive generations of philosophers, social reformers, and historians. In this well-informed and highly insightful essay, a renowned scholar of the Revolution, Robert R. Palmer, formerly of Yale University, explores some of these myths—for instance, that the Revolution was "un-French" in character or, on the contrary, that it was "solely" French—and suggests that often myth and fact cannot be effectively untangled. Along the way, Palmer gauges the Revolution's stunning influence on world history, an impact that continues to be felt today and that will likely be felt for generations to come.

The Revolution quieted down after 1800, but it could not be forgotten. It became lodged in the collective memory, a past event with which each succeeding generation had to come to terms. Some lived in fear, and others in hope, that the giant was only sleeping and might be rearoused. Whether looking backward or forward in time, some thought of the Revolution with awe, some with loathing; some saw in it a means of salvation, others the work of diabolical forces, whether retrospectively in the years before 1800, or prospectively as a possibility of the future. The Revolution became a subject of both myth and history. The two were not opposites; each contributed to the growth of the other. . . .

Excerpted from pages 251–70 of *The World of the French Revolution*, by Robert R. Palmer. Copyright ©1971 by Robert R. Palmer. Reprinted by permission of HarperCollins Publishers, Inc.

## Was the Revolution a Failure?

A persistent lesser myth held that the French Revolution was somehow "un-French." . . . It went back to the most extreme of the original French counterrevolutionaries, and could be found in [the writings of the eighteenth-century English statesman] Edmund Burke, who observed in 1793 that some 30,000 émigrés were the real people of France, and the Revolutionaries only burglars who bad broken into the house. . . . Similar ideas were held by the most ardent partisans of the Bourbon restoration after 1814 [two members of the Bourbon family, Louis XVI's brothers, Louis XVIII and Charles X, were restored to power between 1814 and 1830]. The refutation of this myth produced the first serious histories of the Revolution in the 1820s.

Another long-lived myth held that the French Revolution had been a failure. One version contrasted it to the American Revolution, which was said to have been successful because it was limited in its aims. This idea . . . reappeared in the 1960s in the writings of Hannah Arendt, an American of German philosophical background, who thought that the French Revolution had "failed" because it was disoriented by a blind and futile mass revolt against poverty. A version on the Left held that the Revolution had been "betrayed" by the bourgeoisie. In the allegation of failure there was at least some spark of truth. The Revolution did not fulfill all the claims that it made or all the expectations that it aroused. The middle-class leaders did not satisfy, and in a sense "betrayed," their working-class allies of 1793. They did not thereby betray the actual Revolution, which was mainly a middle-class or bourgeois movement, as the most judicious Marxists have always insisted. The Revolution that they "betrayed," if any, was a timeless Revolution aimed at total emancipation, or a later Revolution carried on in the name of the workers in an industrialized society. The Revolution succeeded in dislodging the monarchy, the nobility, the church, and the sociolegal structures of the Old Order. It introduced a new and modern form of state. It had its failures, its compromises, and its deceptions; but to call it simply a "failure" is to judge by utopian standards. . . .

A related myth, and a less empty one, is the idea that the Revolution was not worth the effort and suffering that it involved. In half a century after 1789, according to this idea, conditions in France would have been much the same, no worse, or possibly even better, if there had been no revolution at all. It is pointed out that the people of Paris, plagued by early industrialism, irresponsible capitalism, inhuman working conditions, mounting population, and increasingly congested and unsanitary streets and lodgings, had more to suffer in 1840 than in 1780. It is noted that the Revolution left wounds and divisions that were not yet healed over a century later, that warring camps were bent on each other's extermination, that every regime into the twentieth century proved unstable, that the national consensus was irreparably broken. Even granting the force of such observations—which are exaggerated . . . — they are not altogether relevant to the question of whether the Revolution was worth the cost. The only way to answer this question is to think in terms of alternatives to the 1780s. . . .

What else could or should have been done, given the breakdown of the royal finances in 1786, the demands of the privileged orders in 1789, the invasion as announced in the Brunswick Manifesto of 1792? . . . Would the Estates General in three houses, as desired by the nobility and by Louis XVI in June, 1789, have known how to govern wisely, or been still governing in 1840? . . . If they could not govern, or if the country would not accept so great a role for nobles and clergy, by what gradual and peaceful means could they have been liquidated or transformed? No positive answer can be given to such questions. All we know is that such questions received an answer in the Revolution. It is possible to see the Revolution as a tragedy. It is not possible to see it as merely foolish, useless, or vain. That the cost was high is a matter of history. The worth of the outlay touches on the realm of myth. For some, it was an appalling waste. For others, the very cost of the Revolution enhanced its value.

## The Outcome of a Long Conflict?

There was an element of myth also, or at least of gross exaggeration, in the memory of the Revolution as having been most especially an attack on Christianity and on all religion. It was forgotten that many Catholic priests had been actual revolutionaries in France, Italy, Poland, and Ireland, and that Protestant ministers in America had refrained from condemning the French Revolution, and in Ireland had joined the rebellion. That both Pope Pius VII himself, and the New England pontiff Jedidiah Morse, had expressed sympathy for revolutionary republicanism disappeared into the "non-facts" of history. What had been a conflict among Christians was seen as a struggle between Christians and infidels. . . .

There were also myths more favorable to the Revolution. Against the idea of the Revolution as "un-French," current during the Restoration, liberal historians pictured it as the most essentially French thing in the long history of France. For them it was the revolt of the "nation" against the privileged classes. This view went back at least to Sieyès' famous pamphlet of 1789 in which the third estate was identified with the nation, and the nobles were dismissed as a useless minority. Liberal historians saw it also as the outcome of a conflict extending over centuries, from the rise of towns and an urban, or burgher, culture in the Middle Ages. In this view . . . the whole history of France, for centuries before 1789, was a struggle between two classes, the people and the nobility, a class war of which the Revolution had been the final battle. . . .

The Revolution became a point in a long continuum, the result of causes reaching far back in time and accumulating over the centuries. Many generations of French history had gone into producing it. Given French history, it had been inevitable. Possibly this myth was mistaken; possibly more immediate and short-run causes offer a better explanation; possibly the Revolution need not have happened. . . .

## Forming a New Revolutionary Mentality

But if the Revolution was only a point in a long process, why should the process stop? Was it possible to believe, in the 1820s and 1830s, that the whole people of France or any other country had been liberated? If not, who had been lib-

erated, and who remained to be liberated in the future? . . .
It was answers given to such questions that also produced
the most potent myth of all, the myth of the continuing or
permanent revolution.

Some of the activists of the 1790s were still alive thirty
years later, and some of these were still militant. Such a
thing as the professional revolutionary had developed, the
man who makes a career of planning and working for revolution, in a way hardly known in the actual French Revolution, when the participants had improvised roles which they
had not foreseen and for which they were unprepared.
Among the survivors of the real Revolutionaries was Filippo
Buonarroti. . . . In 1828 he published a book, part history,
part recollection, in effect a narrative of the French Revolution. . . . The book argued that Robespierre had meant to introduce a kind of socialism or social democracy in 1794 [and]
that he was cut down and put to death for that reason. . . .
Buonarroti's work had a great influence. It was widely read
by the rising generation of socialists in France. It was immediately translated into English. . . . Even those who rejected
its "communism" formed the impression that a true democracy had once almost been realized, only to be betrayed, that
the great Revolution had been rudely interrupted, and that
it ought to continue. . . .

Socialists, republicans, workers, and intellectuals formed
their conception of recent history from such readings. A favorable idea of Robespierre spread among German republicans, and could be found in Russia, at the very beginning of
the Russian revolutionary movement, in the writings of Be-
linski as early as 1842. . . .

The creation of a whole new social vocabulary, unknown
in the French Revolution, revealed that a new revolutionary
mentality was being formed. From Saint-Simon came the
word *avant-garde*, to signify a small elite who would guide a
phlegmatic mass into a regenerated world of the future. The
word soon caught on both in revolutionary politics and in
the arts. . . . "Left" and "Right" came into use, signifying
positive and negative attitudes toward continuing movement
in a revolutionary direction. Above all, the indispensable new

words were "bourgeois" and "proletarian." . . . [The French Revolution] was now seen as a bourgeois revolution leading only to bourgeois democracy in which the bourgeoisie had been liberated but not the working man. . . .

The word "bourgeois" was ambiguous from the beginning. It was a useful term, when used to designate a social stratum that belonged neither to the aristocracy nor to the common people, a stratum of persons in the professions, in trade or government employment, men of education and accepted position, with more or less secure incomes from personal earnings or profits or annuities or the rental of land. Such persons had in fact been the main supporters of the Revolution of the 1790s in all European countries.

But "bourgeois" had other meanings when launched in the 1830s. One might look "down" on the bourgeois as philistine, vulgar, or lacking in the sensibilities of a true upper class. One might look "up" to him as a boss, or person enjoying undue economic advantages and hence a superior way of life. Or, for [German socialist writer] Karl Marx, the bourgeois was anyone, vulgar or refined, noble or plebeian, who owned capital goods as his private property and made a profit from the employment of labor. Briefly, the bourgeois was the designated target of the next revolution.

## A Revolution That Never Came?

The coming revolution was announced in the *Communist Manifesto*, which Marx and [German socialist Friedrich] Engels published [in 1848]. . . . The *Communist Manifesto* heralded a much greater revolution which never came—or which came only in Russia, much later and under different conditions. In form a summons to a grand final Revolution, in substance the *Communist Manifesto*, like Marx's later work, was an analysis of existing or bourgeois society. . . . After the bourgeois revolution a proletarian [workers'] revolution must surely follow.

Whatever other valid message it might contain, the myth of a continuing or proletarian revolution was awkwardly related to historical fact. The supposedly coming revolution was to be made by a beaten-down and oppressed class, virtually excluded from civilized society, but instructed and led by an alert vanguard or elite, who at the proper moment would take power, perhaps peacefully, from the enfeebled hands of a disappearing bourgeoisie, proclaim the public ownership of the means of production, and introduce real liberty and equality while dispensing with political authority, the state itself eventually withering away. . . .

What continued in the nineteenth century was less the Revolution than the idealization of the Revolution. There were indeed the revolutions of 1848 in many countries, and in France the Paris Commune of 1871. All soon succumbed; but the very triumph of counterrevolution, the ferocity with which desperate workingmen and eager republicans were suppressed, kept alive a revolutionary frame of mind. . . . Gradually, by the close of the nineteenth century, with the development of industry, the rise of wages, the softening of the worst social dislocations, and the admission of the working classes to a more or less democratic electorate, the forces making for a real revolution became weaker than ever. Marx and Engels were hardly dead when "revisionism" and "opportunism" appeared among Marxists. The revolutionary mentality, by the turn of the century, signified less an actual expectation of revolution than an inveterate hostility to bourgeois society. It showed itself in the tendency to see everything as an aspect of the class struggle, in a kind of negativism or social alienation, a proud outsider's psychology, an attitude of suspicion, a dislike of conciliation or compromise, a scorn for mere reforms or half-measures or improvements of detail, a contempt for institutions which the Revolution ought to eradicate—though it never did. Even so, the supposedly Marxist or revolutionary workers rallied to their respective governments in the First World War. The myth of a coming proletarian revolution proved less strong than the appeals of national solidarity and self-defense.

In 1918, a few months after the October Revolution in Russia, a statue of Robespierre was erected near the Kremlin [in Moscow]. Made of temporary materials, it soon fell to pieces, and was not replaced. The absence of a more permanent statue suggests that, once the Russian Revolution was clearly established as a reality, it had less need to celebrate distant predecessors in far-away countries. That Robespierre was thus commemorated at all, in 1918, signifies Lenin's belief that his own movement, mediated through Marxism, was descended from the great French Revolution of 1789. . . .

The memory or myth of the French Revolution contributed to the form taken by the revolution in Russia. Without it, Lenin might have become discouraged in the twenty years preceding 1917. With it, he could believe in a long-continuing Revolution, a wave of the future drawing strength from the past—a cause, which however suppressed or deflected by its enemies or betrayed or weakened by its friends, must yet prevail because it embodied the true meaning of history. . . .

## Only in France?

There remains one more myth, which . . . may throw light on these questions. It is the opposite of the conservative myth that the Revolution of 1789 was un-French. This myth holds that the French Revolution was not only French, but French alone. It asserts that there was nothing worth calling a revolution in any other country. It denies the reality of an all-European revolutionary movement in the eighteenth century. It rejects what the French historian Jacques Godechot has called the "Atlantic" revolution, and looks with suspicion on the idea of . . . a revolutionary disturbance common to Europe and America, or to what then constituted Western civilization. In this myth, it is feared that the French Revolution may lose its significance, or be reduced or not seen in its true dimensions, if represented as part of a wider upheaval or allowed to evaporate into a vague international agitation. Like the other myths that have now been surveyed, this one contains its element of historical truth. The French Revolution, like all human events, had its unique features. It was far more revolutionary than the revolutions or attempted revolutions in other countries. But the myth of the purely or exclusively French Revolution is restrictive and confining. The French Revolution becomes greater, not smaller, when seen as part of a larger whole. And the wave of excitement that swept through Europe and America is more understandable when seen as more than a reaction to French events. . . .

Yet somehow the belief arose that no significant revolution had occurred except in France. This became the dominant recollection, or "myth," of later times. It arose from many sources, one of which was among the Revolutionaries themselves.

In 1793, when the French were beset by the Coalition, no other people offered any support. There might be objection to the war, as there was in Britain, Holland, Prussia, and the Austrian empire, but nothing happened; the French were isolated in their crisis, and many of them, including Robespierre, developed a scorn for so-called revolutionaries' and sympathizers in other countries, and a pride in the French as the only people who had the power, courage, or stamina to repel the combined forces of the Old Order of Europe. . . . The idea grew up that each people must rely on itself to make its own revolution. The Revolutionary idea of the "nation" itself promoted this tendency.

Where revolution failed, or where the older institutions maintained themselves against radical opposition, it was convenient not to keep certain memories alive. A failed revolution was not a revolution. What had happened in Ireland in 1798 was a Rebellion. What had happened in Poland in 1794 was an Insurrection. As feelings of nationality and national loyalty became stronger in the nineteenth century, it became a matter of shame and embarrassment, or of actual disbelief, that one's ancestors should have collaborated with foreigners, or even expressed enthusiasm for a French Revolution. Even the democrats of later times suppressed such memories. That there had been many angry "Jacobins" in England and Scotland was forgotten. The enthusiasm in the United States for the French Republic was recalled as a mere passing craze. Only a few hotheads or firebrands, among the Dutch, Belgians, Germans, Swiss, and Italians, could have ever collaborated with the French or invited them into their countries. . . . The myth of a continuing revolution was countered by a myth of continuing indifference to revolutionary temptations, by a myth of a solidarity of separate nations which had hardly existed at the time of the French Revolution. . . .

History became divided into separate national compartments. The French historians had their French Revolution. Others had the respective tribulations of their own countries at that period, or, more often, thought the period of little importance in their own national histories, and wrote very little about it. . . .

## Waves Set in Motion in 1789

But there is no conflict between the ideas of a "distinctively" French Revolution and a wave of revolution throughout Europe and America at the same time.

The main sympathizers with the Revolution everywhere were of the middle classes, those free from the demands of daily menial labor, enjoying the benefits of education and income, yet outside the privileged, aristocratic, patrician, religious, or other favored categories of the Old Order. Often joined by individual noblemen, and often supported by lesser people, they were lawyers and government employees, doctors and pharmacists, merchants and sometimes bankers, men of scientific or technical interests, shopkeepers and manufacturers, professors and teachers, writers and miscellaneous intellectuals, journalists and publishers, occasionally agriculturists and frequently men drawing income from landed rents, together with the sons of those too busy, too elderly, or too prudent to engage in risky agitations themselves. They were, in fact, a revolutionary bourgeoisie.

They not only rebelled; they projected a new form of state and society. They brought the Enlightenment into practical politics. . . . [They] set up the sovereignty of the people. In place of the subject, the Revolutionaries envisaged the citizen, and indeed they created the very idea of national citizenship. They wanted freedom of thought, expression, religion, association, and of enterprise of all kinds, including economic. Against older restraints they affirmed the value of liberty, against old forms of discrimination they made an ideal of equality, and in solidarity with each other, and with all who would join them, they were generous enough to dream of fraternity. They recognized their own program in the great Declaration of Rights of 1789. New rights, for more people, have been demanded ever since. Resistance to new rights has also been a continuing story. The waves set in motion in 1789 have sometimes been stormy, sometimes more tranquil, but never quite calm—nor does it seem likely that they will ever wholly subside.

# Appendix

## Excerpts from Original Documents Pertaining to the French Revolution

### Document 1: Locke Questions the Authority of Absolute Monarchs

*One of the leading influences on the enlightened political and social views of eighteenth-century Europe, English philosopher John Locke (1632–1704) set forth ideas about human freedom and equality that the leaders of both the American and French Revolutions took to heart. In this excerpt from his famous* Second Treatise of Civil Government *(1690), he makes his case that the system of absolute monarchy has no basis in the consent of the governed and is inconsistent with the concept of a civil society.*

Man being born, as has been proved, with a title to perfect freedom, and an uncontrouled enjoyment of all the rights and privileges of the law of nature, equally with any other man, or number of men in the world, hath by nature a power, not only to preserve his property, that is, his life, liberty and estate, against the injuries and attempts of other men; but to judge of, and punish the breaches of that law in others, as he is persuaded the offence deserves, even with death itself, in crimes where the heinousness of the fact, in his opinion, requires it. But because no *political society* can be, nor subsist, without having in itself the power to preserve the property, and in order thereunto, punish the offences of all those of that society; there, and there only is *political society*, where every one of the members hath quitted this natural power, resigned it up into the hands of the community in all cases that exclude him not from appealing for protection to the law established by it. And thus all private judgment of every particular member being excluded, the community comes to be umpire, by settled standing rules, indifferent, and the same to all parties; and by men having authority, from the community, for the execution of those rules, decides all the differences that may happen between any members of that society concerning any matter of right; and punishes those offences which any member hath committed against the society, with such penalties as the law has established: whereby it is easy to discern, who are, and who are not, in *political society* together. Those who are united into one body, and have a common

established law and judicature to appeal to, with authority to decide controversies between them, and punish offenders, are in *civil
society* one with another: but those who have no such common appeal, I mean on earth, are still in the state of nature, each being,
where there is no other, judge for himself, and executioner; which
is, as I have before shewed it, the perfect *state of nature.* . . .

Where-ever therefore any number of men are so united into
one society, as to quit every one his executive power of the law of
nature, and to resign it to the public, there and there only is a *political, or civil society*. And this is done, where-ever any number of
men, in the state of nature, enter into society to make one people,
one body politic, under one supreme government; or else when
any one joins himself to, and incorporates with any government already made: for hereby he authorizes the society, or which is all
one, the legislative thereof, to make laws for him, as the public
good of the society shall require; to the execution whereof, his own
assistance (as to his own decrees) is due. And this *puts men* out of a
state of nature *into* that of a *common-wealth*, by setting up a judge
on earth, with authority to determine all the controversies, and redress the injuries that may happen to any member of the common-
wealth; which judge is the legislative, or magistrates appointed by
it. And where-ever there are any number of men, however associated, that have no such decisive power to appeal to, there they are
still in *the state of nature*.

Hence it is evident, that *absolute monarchy*, which by some men
is counted the only government in the world, is indeed *inconsistent
with civil society*, and so can be no form of civil-government at all:
for the *end of civil society*, being to avoid, and remedy those incon-
veniences of the state of nature, which necessarily follow from
every man's being judge in his own case, by setting up a known authority, to which every one of that society may appeal upon any injury received, or controversy that may arise, and which every one
of the society ought to obey; where-ever any persons are, who have
not such an authority to appeal to, for the decision of any difference between them, there those persons are still *in the state of nature*; and so is every *absolute prince*, in respect of those who are
under his *dominion*.

For he being supposed to have all, both legislative and executive
power in himself alone, there is no judge to be found, no appeal lies
open to any one, who may fairly, and indifferently, and with authority decide, and from whose decision relief and redress may be
expected of any injury or inconveniency, that may be suffered from

the prince, or by his order: so that such a man, however intitled, *Czar*, or *Grand Seignior*, or how you please, is as much *in the state of nature*, with all under his dominion, as he is with the rest of mankind: for where-ever any two men are, who have no standing rule, and common judge to appeal to on earth, for the determination of controversies of right betwixt them, there they are still *in the state of nature*, and under all the inconveniencies of it, with only this woful difference to the subject, or rather slave of an absolute prince: that whereas, in the ordinary state of nature, he has a liberty to judge of his right, and according to the best of his power, to maintain it; now, whenever his property is invaded by the will and order of his monarch, he has not only no appeal, as those in society ought to have, but as if he were degraded from the common state of rational creatures, is denied a liberty to judge of, or to defend his right; and so is exposed to all the misery and inconveniencies, that a man can fear from one, who being in the unrestrained state of nature, is yet corrupted with flattery, and armed with power.

For he that thinks *absolute power purifies men's blood*, and corrects the baseness of human nature, need read but the history of this, or any other age, to be convinced of the contrary. He that would have been insolent and injurious in the woods of *America*, would not probably be much better in a throne; where perhaps learning and religion shall be found out to justify all that he shall do to his subjects, and the sword presently silence all those that dare question it.

Diane Ravitch and Abigail Thernstrom, eds., *The Democracy Reader*. New York: HarperCollins, 1992, pp. 38–40.

## Document 2: Voltaire Calls for Religious Tolerance

*Influential French philosopher-writer Voltaire (François-Marie Arouet, 1694–1778) argued in his 1763* Treatise on Toleration, *excerpted here, that all people should be able to practice their chosen religion without fear of persecution.*

I venture to think that some enlightened and magnanimous minister, some humane and wise prelate, some prince who puts his interest in the number of his subjects and his glory in their welfare, may deign to glance at this inartistic and defective paper. . . .

We have Jews at Bordeaux and Metz and in Alsace; we have Lutherans, Molinists,[1] and Jansenists[2]; can we not suffer and control Calvinists on much the same terms as those on which Catholics are tolerated at London [who did not enjoy political rights but

1. Molinists: adherents to variant Jesuit theology attacked by Dominicans and Jansenists
2. Jansenists: reformist Roman Catholic sect condemned as heretical

could practice their religion]? The more sects there are, the less danger in each. Multiplicity enfeebles them. They are all restrained by just laws which forbid disorderly meetings, insults, and sedition, and are ever enforced by the community.

We know that many fathers of families, who have made large fortunes in foreign lands, are ready to return to their country [the Calvinist refugees]. They ask only the protection of natural law, the validity of their marriages, security as to the condition of their children, the right to inherit from their fathers, and the enfranchisement of their persons. They ask not for public chapels, or the right to municipal offices and dignities. Catholics have not these things in England and other countries. It is not a question of giving immense privileges and secure positions to a faction, but of allowing a peaceful people to live, and of moderating the laws once, but no longer, necessary. It is not our place to tell the ministry what is to be done; we do but ask consideration for the unfortunate. . . .

The great means to reduce the number of fanatics, if any remain, is to submit that disease of the mind to the treatment of reason, which slowly, but infallibly, enlightens men. Reason is gentle and humane. It inspires liberality, suppresses discord, and strengthens virtue; it has more power to make obedience to the laws attractive than force has to compel. . . .

Natural law is that indicated to men by nature. . . . Human law must in every case be based on natural law. All over the earth the great principle of both is: Do not unto others what you would that they do not unto you. Now, in virtue of this principle, one man cannot say to another: "Believe what I believe, and what thou canst not believe, or thou shalt perish." Thus do men speak in Portugal, Spain, and Goa. In some other countries they are now content to say: "Believe, or I detest thee; believe, or I will do thee all the harm I can. Monster, thou sharest not my religion, and therefore hast no religion; thou shalt be a thing of horror to thy neighbours, thy city, and thy province."

If it were a point of human law to behave thus, the Japanese should detest the Chinese, who should abhor the Siamese; the Siamese, in turn, should persecute the Tibetans, who should fall upon the Hindus. A Mogul should tear out the heart of the first Malabarian[3] he met; the Malabarian should slay the Persian, who might massacre the Turk; and all of them should fling themselves against the Christians, who have so long devoured each other.

3. Malabarian: Indian Christians recognizing as supreme authority the Syrian Orthodox patriarch, not the pope

The supposed right of intolerance is absurd and barbaric. It is the right of the tiger; nay, it is far worse, for tigers do but tear in order to have food, while we rend each other for paragraphs.

Lynn Hunt, ed., *The French Revolution and Human Rights: A Brief Documentary History*. Boston: St. Martin's Press, 1996, pp. 39–40.

## Document 3: French Working Women Seek Recognition

*This excerpt from the "Petition of Women of the Third Estate to the King," presented to Louis XVI in January 1789, lists the grievances of a group that made up a large segment of French society. Hoping to benefit from the reforms of the upcoming Estates General, working women asked for better educational and work opportunities, which they claimed would make them better workers, wives, and mothers, and that they not be identified as or confused with disreputable women, namely prostitutes.*

Sire,

At a time when the different orders of the state are occupied with their interests; when everyone seeks to make the most of his titles and rights; when some anxiously recall the centuries of servitude and anarchy, while others make every effort to shake off the last links that still bind them to the imperious remains of feudalism; women—continual objects of the admiration and scorn of men—could they not also make their voices heard midst this general agitation?

Excluded from the national assemblies by laws so well consolidated that they allow no hope of infringement, they do not ask, Sire, for your permission to send their deputies to the Estates General; they know too well how much favor will play a part in the election, and how easy it would be for those elected to impede the freedom of voting.

We prefer, Sire, to place our cause at your feet; not wishing to obtain anything except from your heart, it is to it that we address our complaints and confide our miseries.

The women of the Third Estate are almost all born without wealth; their education is very neglected or very defective: it consists in their being sent to school with a teacher who himself does not know the first word of the language [Latin] he teaches. They continue to go there until they can read the service of the Mass in French and Vespers in Latin. Having fulfilled the first duties of religion, they are taught to work; having reached the age of fifteen or sixteen, they can earn five or six *sous* a day. If nature has refused them beauty they get married, without a dowry, to unfortunate artisans; lead aimless, difficult lives stuck in the provinces; and give birth to children they are incapable of raising. If, on the contrary, they are born pretty, without breeding, without principles, with no idea of morals, they become the prey of the first seducer, commit a first sin, come to Paris to bury their shame, end by losing it altogether [i.e., become prostitutes], and die victims of dissolute ways. . . .

To prevent so many ills, Sire, we ask that men not be allowed, under any pretext, to exercise trades that are the prerogative of women—whether as seamstress, embroiderer, millinery shopkeeper, etc., etc.; if we are left at least with the needle and the spindle, we promise never to handle the compass or the square.

We ask, Sire, that your benevolence provide us with the means of making the most of the talents with which nature will have endowed us, notwithstanding the impediments which are forever being placed on our education.

May you assign us positions, which we alone will be able to fill, which we will occupy only after having passed a strict examination, following trustworthy inquiries concerning the purity of our morals.

We ask to be enlightened, to have work, not in order to usurp men's authority, but in order to be better esteemed by them, so that we might have the means of living safe from misfortune and so that poverty does not force the weakest among us, who are blinded by luxury and swept along by example, to join the crowd of unfortunate women [prostitutes] who overpopulate the streets and whose *debauched* audacity disgraces our sex and the men who keep them company.

We would wish this class of women might wear a mark of identification. Today, when they adopt even the modesty of our dress, when they mingle everywhere in all kinds of clothing, we often find ourselves confused with them; some men make mistakes and make us blush because of their scorn. They should never be able to take off the identification under pain of working in public workshops for the benefit of the poor (it is known that work is the greatest punishment that can be inflicted on them). . . . However, it occurs to us that the empire of fashion would be destroyed and one would run the risk of seeing many too many women dressed in the same color.

We implore you, Sire, to set up free schools where we might learn our language on the basis of principles, religion and ethics. May one and the other be offered to us in all their grandeur, entirely stripped of the petty applications which attenuate their majesty; may our hearts be formed there; may we be taught above

all to practice the virtues of our sex: gentleness, mode
charity. . . .

We ask to take leave of ignorance, to give our children a sound
and reasonable education so as to make of them subjects worthy of
serving you. We will teach them to cherish the beautiful name of
Frenchmen; we will transmit to them the love we have for Your
Majesty. For we are certainly willing to leave valor and genius to
men, but we will always challenge them over the dangerous and
precious gift of sensibility; we defy them to love you better than we
do. They run to Versailles, most of them for their interests, while
we, Sire, go to see you there, and when with difficulty and with
pounding hearts, we can gaze for an instance upon your August
Person, tears flow from our eyes. The idea of Majesty, of the Sovereign, vanishes, and we see in you only a tender Father, for whom
we would give our lives a thousand times.

Lynn Hunt, ed., *The French Revolution and Human Rights: A Brief Documentary History*. Boston: St. Martin's Press, 1996, pp. 60–63.

## Document 4: A People Ready for Reform

*In the spring of 1789, groups all over France drew up* cahiers, *lists of grievances, which they expected would be addressed in the upcoming Estates General. This tract from the "Cahier of the Third Estate of the City of Paris" invokes the concepts of natural civil and religious liberties, reflecting the strong influence of liberal philosophers like Locke and Montesquieu. Clearly, the people were ready for, and indeed not likely to settle for less than, sweeping reforms.*

### Preliminary Observations

We insist that our representatives resist with the utmost determination everything which may offend the dignity of free citizens
who have exercised the sovereign rights of the nation.

Public opinion appears to have recognized the necessity for deliberation by head to compensate for the disadvantages of distinction of orders, to allow public spirit to prevail, and to make the
adoption of good laws easier.

The representatives of the city of Paris must remember the
firmness they are to exercise on this point; they must regard it as a
strict right, as the subject of a special mandate.

They are especially enjoined not to consent to any tax or any
loan, unless the declaration of the nation's rights has passed into
law, and unless the first principles of the Constitution have been
agreed and assured.

This first duty fulfilled, they shall proceed to the verification of the public debt and to its consolidation.

They shall demand that every subject of major importance shall be deliberated on twice, at intervals appropriate to the importance of the questions, and shall only be decided by an absolute majority of voices, that is to say by more than half the votes.

**Declaration of Rights**

In every political society, all men are equal in rights.

All power emanates from the nation, and may only be exercised for its wellbeing.

The general will makes the law; public might ensures its execution.

The nation alone can grant supply; it has the right to determine the amount, to limit its duration, to apportion it, to assign its use, to demand an account of it and to insist on its publication.

Law exists only to guarantee to each individual the ownership of his property and the safety of his person.

All property is inviolable. No citizen may be arrested or punished except by legal judgment.

No citizen, not even a soldier, may be dismissed without a hearing.

Every citizen has the right to be admitted to any employment, profession or dignity.

The natural, civil, and religious liberty of each man, his personal safety, his absolute independence of every other authority except that of the law, debars all enquiry into his opinions, speech, writings, and actions, provided that they do not disturb public order, and do not encroach on the rights of others.

D.I. Wright, ed., *The French Revolution: Introductory Documents*. St. Lucia: University of Queensland Press, 1974, pp. 30–31.

## Document 5: Creation of the National Assembly

*The following is excerpted from the memoirs, published after the Revolution, of Jean-Sylvain Bailley, one of the leaders of the third estate and later a president of the National Assembly. Bailley records Abbé Sieyès's call on June 17, 1789, for the nobles and clergy to join the commoners in forming the Assembly, as well as the Assembly's opening declaration, which claimed that no other body legitimately represented the general will of the nation.*

The assembly had no other resort than to summon the two privileged chambers to the hall of the States for the ratification of powers in common. Consequently he [Sieyès] proposed the following resolution:

"The assembly of the commons, deliberating on the overture of conciliation proposed by the commissioners of the king, has deemed it incumbent on it to take at the same time into consideration the resolution which the nobility have hastened to adopt respecting the same overture. . . .

"It is of the opinion that it is an urgent duty for the representatives of the nation, to whatever class of citizens they belong, to form themselves, without further delay, into an active assembly, capable of commencing and fulfilling the object of their mission. The assembly directs the commissioners who attended the various conferences, called conciliatory, to draw up a report of the long and vain efforts of the deputies of the commons to bring back the classes of the privileged to true principles; it takes upon itself the exposition of the motives which oblige it to pass from a state of expectation to a state of action; finally, it resolves that this report and these motives shall be printed at the head of the present deliberation.

"But, since it is not possible to form themselves into an active assembly without previously recognizing those who have a right to compose it—that is to say, those who are qualified to vote as representatives of the nation—the same deputies of the commons deem it their duty to make a last trial with the clergy and the nobility, who claim the same quality, but have nevertheless refused up to the present moment to make themselves recognized. . . .

"In consequence, and from the necessity which the representatives of the nation are under to proceed to business, the deputies of the commons entreat you anew, gentlemen, and their duty enjoins them to address to you, as well individually as collectively, a last summons to come to the hall of the States, to attend, concur in, and submit, like themselves, to the common verification of powers.". . .

A *yes* and *no* vote was taken by roll call, and the motion of the Abbe Sieyès was adopted by a large majority. Here is the resolution that was adopted and which is the first constitutional act:

"The Assembly, deliberating after the verification of powers, ascertains that it is already composed of representatives sent directly by ninety-six hundredths, at least, of the nation. . . .

"Moreover, as it belongs only to the verified representatives to concur in the national will, and as all the verified representatives are to be admitted into this Assembly, it is further indispensable to conclude that it belongs to it, and to it alone, to interpret and to represent the general will of the nation.

"There cannot exist any veto, any negative power, between the throne and the Assembly.

"The Assembly therefore declares that the general labor of the national restoration can and ought to be begun by the deputies present, and that they ought to prosecute it without interruption and without impediment.

"The denomination of *National Assembly* is the only one suitable to the Assembly in the present state of things, as well because the members who compose it are the only representatives legitimately and publicly known and verified, as because they are sent by nearly the whole of the nation; and lastly because, the representation being one and indivisible, none of the deputies, for whatever order or class he has been elected, has the right to exercise those functions separately from this Assembly.

"The Assembly will never relinquish the hope of collecting in its bosom all the deputies who are now absent; it will not cease to call them to fulfill the obligation imposed upon them to concur in the holding of the States-General. At whatever moment the absent deputies present themselves during the session that is about to be opened, it declares beforehand that it will be ready to receive them, and to share with them, after the verification of their powers, the series of important labors which are to accomplish the regeneration of France.

"The National Assembly decrees that the reasons for the present resolution be immediately drawn up, to be presented to the king and to the nation."

This resolution agreed upon, the Assembly voted to apprise the king of it in a respectful address, and the room resounded with repeated cries of "Long live the King!"

E.L. Higgins, ed., *The French Revolution as Told by Contemporaries*. Boston: Houghton Mifflin, 1939, pp. 81–83.

## Document 6: The Tennis Court Oath

*On June 20, 1789, finding themselves locked out of the hall in which they had met on previous days, the Assembly deputies retired to a nearby tennis court and swore the now famous oath, reproduced here, not to disband under any circumstances until they had created a national constitution.*

The National Assembly, considering that it has been summoned to determine the constitution of the Kingdom, to contrive the regeneration of law and order, and to maintain true principles of monarchy; that nothing can prevent it from pursuing its deliberations in whatever place it may be forced to establish itself, and, finally, that wherever its members are gathered, there is the National Assembly;

Decrees that all members of this Assembly shall immediately swear a solemn oath not to separate, and to re-assemble wherever circumstances may necessitate, until the constitution of the Kingdom is established and consolidated on sound foundations. The said oath sworn, all members, and each of them severally, shall ratify by signature this unshakable resolution.

D.I. Wright, ed., *The French Revolution: Introductory Documents*. St. Lucia: University of Queensland Press, 1974, pp. 39–40.

## Document 7: Lafayette's Declaration of Rights

*The Marquis de Lafayette (1757–1834) earned a reputation as a hero for aiding the American rebels in their war for independence in the 1770s. He also served as a deputy of the nobility in the Estates General but took the side of the third estate. Excerpted here is part of his July 11, 1789, call for a declaration of human rights and his proposed version of such a document, which his friend Thomas Jefferson had helped draft.*

The first [reason for a declaration] is to recall the sentiments that nature has engraved on the heart of every individual and to facilitate the development of them, which is all the more interesting in that, for a nation to love liberty, it suffices that it be acquainted with it, and for it to be free, it suffices that it wishes it.

The second reason is to express these eternal truths from which all institutions should be derived and to become, in the labors of the representatives of the nation, a loyal guide that always leads them back to the source of natural and social right. . . .

The merit of a declaration of rights consists in truth and precision; it should say what everyone knows, what everyone feels. It is only this idea, Sirs, that could have engaged me to offer the draft that I have the honor of presenting to you.

Far be it from me to ask that it be adopted; I ask only that the Assembly have copies made to be distributed in the different subcommittees; this first effort on my part will push other members to present other projects which will better fulfill the wishes of the Assembly, and which I will eagerly prefer to my own.

[Then follows his project, much briefer than the final declaration but sharing many of its general principles.]

Nature has made men free and equal; the distinctions necessary to the social order can only be founded on general utility.

Every man is born with inalienable and imprescriptible rights; these are the freedom of all his opinions; the care of his honor and his life; the right of property; the entire disposition of his own person, his industry, and all his faculties; the communication of his thoughts by all possible means; the pursuit of well-being and resistance to oppression.

The exercise of natural rights has no other limits than those which assure their enjoyment to all other members of society.

No man may be subjected to laws other than those consented to by him or his representatives, previously promulgated and legally applied.

The principle of all sovereignty resides in the nation. . . .

[Five other principles followed.]

Lynn Hunt, ed., *The French Revolution and Human Rights: A Brief Documentary History.* Boston: St. Martin's Press, 1996, pp. 72–73.

## Document 8: The Fall of the Bastille

*This vivid description of the famous surrender of the Bastille to a Paris mob on July 14, 1789, is from the memoirs of French scholar Jean-François Marmontel (1723–1799).*

The Bastille, as a state prison, had always been odious on account of the iniquitous [wicked] use to which the despotism of ministers had applied it under preceding reigns; and, as a fortress, it was formidable, particularly to those populous and mutinous faubourgs [Paris suburbs] which its walls commanded, and which, in their riots, saw themselves under fire of the cannon of its towers. To agitate these multitudes at its will, and make them act boldly, the republican faction then ardently desired that they might be rid of this imposing object. Honest men, even the most peaceful and most enlightened, wished too that the Bastille might be destroyed, because they hated the despotism of which it was the bulwark; and in this wish they consulted their personal security more than their real safety; for the despotism of license is a thousand times more dreadful than that of authority, and the unbridled populace is the most cruel of tyrants. The Bastille, then, should not have been destroyed, but its keys should have been deposited in the sanctuary of the laws. . . .

De Launay [commander of the fortress] had expected to intimidate the crowd; but it is evident that he wished to spare it. He had fifteen pieces of cannon on the towers; and . . . not one single cannon shot was fired from these towers. There were besides, in the interior of the castle, three cannon loaded with case shot, pointed in front of the drawbridge. These would have made great slaughter at the moment when the people came pouring in crowds into the first court; he fired but one, and that but once. He was provided with firearms of every kind. . . . He had procured from the arsenal abundance of ammunition, bullets, fifteen thousand cartridges, and twenty thousand pounds of powder. In fine, he had collected on the two towers of the drawbridge a mass of stones and broken iron, in order to crush the besiegers if they should advance to the foot of the walls. But in all these preparations to sustain a siege, he had forgotten provisions; and shut up in his castle with eighty Invalides [pensioners], thirty-two Swiss soldiers, and his staff, all the store he had on the day of the attack consisted of two sacks of flour and a little rice; a proof that all the rest was only to inspire terror. . . .

The forecourts of the Bastille had been abandoned. Some determined men having dared to break the chains of the drawbridge which barred the entrance into the first court, the people rushed in there in crowds; and deaf to the voice of the soldiers who, from the tops of the towers, forbore to fire on them, and cried out to them to retire, they persisted in advancing towards the walls of the castle. It was then that they were fired upon by the soldiers; and being put to flight, they saved themselves under the covert of the forecourts. One killed and a few wounded spread terror even to the Hôtel de Ville; multitudes came to demand urgently, in the name of the people, that deputations might be resorted to, in order to stop the carnage. Two of these deputations arrived, one by the arsenal, and the other by the side of the Faubourg Saint Antoine. "Advance!" cried the Invalides to them from the tops of the towers. "We will not fire on you; advance with your flag. The governor is going down, the castle bridge will be let down in order to introduce you, and we will give hostages." The white flag was already hoisted on the towers, and the soldiers held their arms inverted in sign of peace. But neither of the deputations dared to advance so far as the last forecourt. At the same time, the crowd was pressing towards the drawbridge and firing from all sides. The besieged then had reason to think that these appearances of deputation were but a trick to surprise them; and after having cried in vain to the people not to advance, they found themselves obliged to fire in their turn.

The people, repulsed a second time, and furious at seeing some of their own body fall under the fire of the fortress, took that revenge in which it usually indulges. The barracks and shops of the forecourt were pillaged; the house of the governor was delivered to the flames. The firing of one cannon, loaded with case shot, and a discharge of musketry had driven back this crowd of robbers and incendiaries; when, at the head of a dozen brave citizens, Élie [a leader of the crowd], advancing to the very edge of the ditch, cried out to the besieged to surrender, promising that not a man should be hurt. He then perceived a hand extended through an opening in a part of the drawbridge and presenting to him a note. This note was received by means of a plank that was held over the ditch; it was written in these words:

> We have twenty thousand pounds of powder. We will blow up the castle if you do not accept our capitulation.
>
> DE LAUNAY.

Élie, after having read the note, cried out that he accepted it; and on the part of the fort, all hostilities ceased. However, De Launay, before he gave himself up to the people, wished that the capitulation should be ratified and signed at the Hôtel de Ville, and that, to secure his own safety and that of his soldiers, an imposing guard should receive and protect them. But the unfortunate Invalides, thinking to hasten their deliverance, did violence to the governor by crying out from the court, " The Bastille surrenders!"

It was then that De Launay, seizing the match of a cannon, threatened to go and set fire to the powder magazine; and perhaps he was firmly resolved to do it. The sentinels who guarded the magazine presented to him their bayonets; and in spite of himself, without further precaution or delay, he saw himself forced to surrender.

E.L. Higgins, ed., *The French Revolution as Told by Contemporaries.* Boston: Houghton Mifflin, 1939, pp. 96–98.

## Document 9: The Great Rights Declaration

*Presented here in its entirety, the Declaration of the Rights of Man and Citizen, adopted by the National Assembly on August 27, 1789, stands, along with the American Declaration of Independence and Bill of Rights, as one of the greatest human rights expressions in history.*

The representatives of the French people, organized in National Assembly, considering that ignorance, forgetfulness or contempt of the rights of man, are the sole causes of the public miseries and of the corruption of governments, have resolved to set forth in a solemn declaration the natural, inalienable, and sacred rights of man, in order that this declaration, being ever present to all the members of the social body, may unceasingly remind them of their rights and their duties; in order that the acts of the legislative power and those of the executive power may be each moment compared with the aim of every political institution and thereby may be more respected; and in order that the demands of citizens, grounded henceforth upon simple and incontestable principles, may always take the direction of maintaining the constitution and welfare of all.

In consequence, the National Assembly recognizes and declares, in the presence and under the auspices of the Supreme Being, the following rights of man and citizen.

1. Men are born and remain free and equal in rights. Social distinctions can be based only upon public utility.
2. The aim of every political association is the preservation of the natural and imprescriptible rights of man. These rights are liberty, property, security, and resistance to oppression.
3. The source of all sovereignty is essentially in the nation; no body, no individual can exercise authority that does not proceed from it in plain terms.
4. Liberty consists in the power to do anything that does not injure others; accordingly, the exercise of the natural rights of each man has no limits except those that secure to the other members of society the enjoyment of these same rights. These limits can be determined only by law.
5. The law has the right to forbid only such actions as are injurious to society. Nothing can be forbidden that is not interdicted by the law, and no one can be constrained to do that which it does not order.
6. Law is the expression of the general will. All citizens have the right to take part personally, or by their representatives, in its formation. It must be the same for all, whether it protects or punishes. All citizens being equal in its eyes, are equally eligible to all public dignities, places, and employments, according to their capacities, and without other distinction than that of their virtues and their talents.
7. No man can be accused, arrested, or detained, except in the cases determined by the law and according to the forms that it has prescribed. Those who procure, expedite, execute, or cause to be executed arbitrary orders ought to be punished: but every citizen summoned or seized in virtue of the law ought to render instant obedience; he makes himself guilty by resistance.
8. The law ought to establish only penalties that are strictly and obviously necessary, and no one can be punished except in virtue of a law established and promulgated prior to the offence and legally applied.
9. Every man being presumed innocent until he has been pronounced guilty, if it is thought indispensable to arrest him, all severity that may not be necessary to secure his person ought to be strictly suppressed by law.

10. No one should be disturbed on account of his opinions, even religious, provided their manifestation does not derange the public order established by law.

11. The free communication of ideas and opinions is one of the most precious of the rights of man; every citizen then can freely speak, write, and print, subject to responsibility for the abuse of this freedom in the cases determined by law.

12. The guarantee of the rights of man and citizen requires a public force; this force then is instituted for the advantage of all and not for the personal benefit of those to whom it is entrusted.

13. For the maintenance of the public force and for the expenses of administration a general tax is indispensable; it ought to be equally apportioned among all the citizens according to their means.

14. All the citizens have the right to ascertain, by themselves or by their representatives, the necessity of the public tax, to consent to it freely, to follow the employment of it, and to determine the quota, the assessment, the collection, and the duration of it.

15. Society has the right to call for an account of his administration from every public agent.

16. Any society in which the guarantee of the rights is not secured, or the separation of powers not determined, has no constitution at all.

17. Property being a sacred and inviolable right, no one can be deprived of it, unless a legally established public necessity evidently demands it, under the condition of a just and prior indemnity.

Diane Ravitch and Abigail Thernstrom, eds., *The Democracy Reader.* New York: HarperCollins, 1992, pp. 54–55.

## Document 10: The Royal Family's Return to Paris

*This account of the forced return of the king and his family from Versailles to Paris on October 6, 1789, is by Marie-Antoinette's foster brother, Joseph Weber, who was living at the French court at the time. Because of his personal tie with the queen, Weber's version of these events is, not surprisingly, sympathetic to the royal family and critical of the Paris mob, which he depicts as ugly and cruel.*

The people, who had given quarter to the *gardes du corps*, did not, for all that, lose sight of the principal object of their enterprise. They demanded, with shrieks, that the king come to Paris; they said that if the royal family would come to Paris to live there would be no lack of provisions. M. de La Fayette seconded this desire with all his might in the council which was then held in the presence of Their Majesties. Finally, the king, fatigued, solicited, and pressed by all, gave his word that he would depart at midday. This promise flew from mouth to mouth; the acclamations of the people and a fusillade [massed firing] of musketry were the results.

His Majesty appeared then for the second time on the balcony to confirm to the people the promise he had just given to M. de La Fayette. At this second appearance, the joy of the populace was unrestrained. A voice demanded "the queen on the balcony." This princess, who was never greater nor more magnanimous than at moments when danger was most imminent, unhesitatingly presented herself on the balcony, holding M. le Dauphin [the young prince] by one hand and Madame Royale [the young princess] by the other. At that a voice cried out, "No children!" The queen, by a backward movement of her arms, pushed the children back into the room, and remained alone on the balcony, folding her hands on her breast, with a countenance showing calmness, nobility, and dignity impossible to describe, and seemed thus to wait for death. This act of resignation astonished the assassins so much and inspired so much admiration in the coarse people that a general clapping of hands and cries of "Bravo! long live the Queen!" repeated on all sides, disconcerted the malevolent. I saw, however, one of these madmen aim at the queen, and his neighbor knock down the barrel of the musket with a blow of his hand, nearly massacring this brigand. . . . [Later that day, on the march toward Paris] one saw first the mass of the Parisian troops file by. Each soldier carried a loaf on the end of his bayonet. Then came the fishwives, drunk with fury, joy, and wine, holding branches of trees ornamented with ribbons, sitting astride the cannon, mounted on the horses of the *gardes du corps*, and wearing their hats. Some disported cuirasses [breastplates] before and behind, and others were armed with sabers and muskets. They were accompanied by the multitude of brigands and Paris laborers. . . . They halted from time to time to fire new salvos, while the fishwives descended from their horses and cannon to march around the carriage of the king. They embraced the soldiers and roared out songs to the refrain of "Here is the baker, the baker's wife, and the baker's little boy!" The horror of a cold, somber, rainy day; the infamous militia splattering through the mud; the harpies, monsters with human faces; the captive monarch and his family ignominiously [shamefully] dragged along surrounded by guards; all formed such a frightful spectacle, such a mixture of shame and anguish, that to this very day I cannot think of it without my senses being completely overwhelmed.

At times the queen was in a state of passive endurance difficult to describe. Her son was on her knees; he suffered hunger and asked for food. Unable to fulfill his desires, Marie Antoinette pressed him to her heart, weeping. She exhorted him to suffer in silence. The young prince became resigned.

E.L. Higgins, ed., *The French Revolution as Told by Contemporaries*. Boston: Houghton Mifflin, 1939, pp. 129–30.

## Document 11: Robespierre Stands Up for Equal Voting Rights

*Although he came to exemplify the brutality and ruthless abuse of power of the Terror, Maximilien Robespierre (1758–1794) began as a fervent advocate of freedom and equality. In his speech of October 22, 1789, to the Assembly, quoted here, he objected to the proposal, supported by a majority of his colleagues, that only the small minority of French citizens with a certain amount of property should have the right to vote. Such restrictions, he declared, blatantly violated the Declaration of Rights only recently passed by the legislature.*

All citizens, whoever they are, have the right to aspire to all levels of officeholding. Nothing is more in line with your declaration of rights, according to which all privileges, all distinctions, all exceptions must disappear. The Constitution establishes that sovereignty resides in the people, in all the individuals of the people. Each individual therefore has the right to participate in making the law which governs him and in the administration of the public good which is his own. If not, it is not true that all men are equal in rights, that every man is a citizen. If he who only pays a tax equivalent to a day of work has fewer rights than he who pays the equivalent to three days of work, and he who pays at the level of ten days has more rights than he whose tax only equals the value of three, then he who enjoys 100,000 *livres* [French pounds] of revenue has 100 times as many rights as he who only has 1,000 *livres* of revenue. It follows from all your decrees that every citizen has the right to participate in making the law and consequently that of being an elector or eligible for office without distinction of wealth.

Lynn Hunt, ed., *The French Revolution and Human Rights: A Brief Documentary History*. Boston: St. Martin's Press, 1996, p. 83.

## Document 12: The Jews Denied Civil Rights

*The following speech, which was first delivered in the National Assembly and then circulated in pamphlet form in the spring of 1790, is the work of the bishop of Nancy, Anne Louis Henri de La Fare, a representative from Lorraine, a province with many Jewish inhabitants. He speaks against giving Jews full civil rights, falling back on age-old anti-Semitic arguments, for instance, that the Jews are foreigners, temporary visitors in France, and therefore not true citizens deserving of rights under the law. Despite the high-minded language of the August 1789 Declaration of Rights, most French leaders were not yet prepared to grant equal rights to everyone; Jews were denied full emancipation until September 1792.*

Thus, Sirs, assure each Jewish individual his liberty, security, and the enjoyment of his property. You owe it to this individual who has strayed into our midst; you owe him nothing more. He is a foreigner to whom, during the time of this passage and his stay, France owes hospitality, protection, and security. But it cannot and should not admit to public posts, to the administration, to the prerogatives of the family a tribe that, regarding itself everywhere as foreign, never exclusively embraces any region; a tribe whose religion, customs, and physical and moral regime essentially differ from that of all other people; a tribe finally whose eyes turn constantly toward the common fatherland [Palestine, the site of ancient Israel] that should one day reunite its dispersed members and which cannot consequently consecrate any solid attachment to the land that supports it. . . .

There are only in France a small number of provinces where Jews have been permitted to establish themselves. The rest of the kingdom has but little or no relationship to the individuals of this nation. Thus, the greater part of the deputies would not know how to judge the present question with sufficient knowledge of the issue. The decision, nonetheless, is of a kind that should not be left to the enthusiasm of the emotions or to the seduction of the mind [presumably by excessively humanitarian leanings]. . . .

There are also moral and local considerations that should, if not guide, then at least enlighten the legislation regarding the Jewish nation.

The prejudices of the people against the Jews are only too well-known. From time to time, they explode into violence: recently in Alsace, some people committed the most criminal excesses against the Jews. A few months ago, similar misfortunes menaced them in Nancy [a city in Lorraine]. People wanted to pillage their houses, mistreat their persons; the animosity was extreme. Did they merit this malevolence because of criminal maneuvers, monopolies, or

ntrary to the interests of the people? No, Sirs: the most
ρ.roach made to them was spreading out too much into
the province, acquiring houses, lands, and privileges that the former laws did not give to them.

From this account it is easy to understand the habitual disposition of the people; it is a fire always ready to be lit. Any extension
that a decree of the National Assembly would hasten to give to the
civil existence of the Jews, before opinion has been prepared in advance and led by degrees to this change, could occasion great dis-
asters. It is only prudent to foresee possible misfortunes; it is only
wise to prevent them.

Lynn Hunt, ed., *The French Revolution and Human Rights: A Brief Documentary History.* Boston: St. Martin's Press, 1996, pp. 97–98.

## Document 13: Noble Titles Abolished

*The decree forbidding anyone from receiving or claiming the age-old ti-
tles of the nobility, issued by the National Assembly on June 19, 1790,
was a logical extension of the August 4, 1789, decrees that had struck
down many of the feudal privileges long enjoyed by the nobles and as such
was part of the ongoing revolutionary transition to a classless society.*

1. Hereditary nobility is abolished forever; accordingly, the titles
   of prince, duke, count, marquis, viscount, *vidame*, baron, knight,
   *messire*, squire, noble, and all other similar titles shall neither be
   accepted by nor bestowed upon anyone whomsoever.
2. A citizen may assume only his real family name; no one may wear
   liveries [distinctive clothing] or have them worn, or have coats of
   arms; incense shall be burned in the churches only to honor the
   Divinity, and shall not be offered to any person whomsoever.
3. The titles of *monseigneur* and *messeigneurs* shall not be bestowed
   upon any group or individual; likewise, the titles of excellency,
   highness, eminence, grace, etc.; but no citizen may be permitted, under pretext of the present decree, to attack the monu-
   ments placed in churches, the charters, titles, and other documents concerning families or properties, or the decorations in
   any public or private place; and the execution of the provisions
   relative to liveries and coats of arms placed upon carriages may
   not be effected or required by anyone whomsoever until 14 July
   for citizens living in Paris, and until three months hence for
   those living in the provinces.
4. The present decree does not apply to foreigners; they may preserve their liveries and coats of arms in France.

John H. Stewart, ed., *A Documentary Survey of the French Revolution.* New York: Macmillan, 1951, pp. 142–43.

## Document 14: An Unsuccessful Plea for Women's Rights

*In July 1790, Marie-Jean, marquis de Condorcet (1743–1794), the well-known French mathematician, philosopher, and member of the Academy of Science, wrote a controversial newspaper article calling on French leaders to extend full civil rights to women. Condorcet, who also lobbied for equal rights for Protestants and Jews and for the abolition of slavery, argued that the doctrine of natural rights, as stated in the August 27, 1789, Declaration of Rights, must apply to all adults regardless of gender and that logically either all humans have the same natural rights or no one has any rights at all. Although his plea was rejected almost out of hand by his colleagues, Condorcet must be respected and admired for his courageous stand; more than any other French revolutionary figure, he was a liberal, progressive thinker ahead of his time.*

Habit can familiarize men with the violation of their natural rights to the point that among those who have lost them no one dreams of reclaiming them or believes that he has suffered an injustice.

Some of these violations even escaped the philosophers and legislators when with the greatest zeal they turned their attention to establishing the common rights of the individuals of the human race and to making those rights the sole foundation of political institutions. For example, have they not all violated the principle of equality of rights by quietly depriving half of mankind of the right to participate in the formation of the laws, by excluding women from the rights of citizenship? Is there a stronger proof of the power of habit even among enlightened men than seeing the principle of equality of rights invoked in favor of three or four hundred men deprived of their rights by an absurd prejudice [perhaps he is thinking of actors here] and at the same time forgetting those rights when it comes to twelve million women?

For this exclusion not to be an act of tyranny one would have to prove that the natural rights of women are not absolutely the same as those of men or show that they are not capable of exercising them. Now the rights of men follow only from the fact that they are feeling beings, capable of acquiring moral ideas and of reasoning about these ideas. Since women have the same qualities, they necessarily have equal rights. Either no individual in mankind has true rights, or all have the same ones; and whoever votes against the right of another, whatever be his religion, his color, or his sex, has from that moment abjured his own rights.

It would be difficult to prove that women are incapable of exercising the rights of citizenship. Why should beings exposed to pregnancies and to passing indispositions not be able to exercise

rights that no one ever imagined taking away from people who
have gout every winter or who easily catch colds? Even granting a
superiority of mind in men that is not the necessary consequence
of the difference in education (which is far from being proved and
which ought to be if women are to be deprived of a natural right
without injustice), this superiority can consist in only two points.
It is said that no woman has made an important discovery in the
sciences or given proof of genius in the arts, letters, etc. But certainly no one would presume to limit the rights of citizenship exclusively to men of genius. Some add that no woman has the same
extent of knowledge or the same power of reasoning as certain
men do; but what does this prove except that the class of very enlightened men is small? There is complete equality between
women and the rest of men; if this little class of men were set aside,
inferiority and superiority would be equally shared between the
two sexes. Now since it would be completely absurd to limit the
rights of citizenship and the eligibility for public offices to this superior class, why should women be excluded rather than those men
who are inferior to a great number of women?

. . . It is said that women have never been guided by what is
called reason despite much intelligence, wisdom, and a faculty for
reasoning developed to the same degree as in subtle dialecticians.
This observation is false: they have not conducted themselves, it is
true, according to the reason of men but rather according to their
own. Their interests not being the same due to the defects of the
laws, the same things not having for them at all the same importance as for us, they can, without being unreasonable, determine
their course of action according to other principles and work toward a different goal. It is as reasonable for a woman to occupy
herself with the embellishment of her person as it was for Demos-
thenes [a Greek orator] to cultivate his voice and gestures.

It is said that women, though better than men in that they are
gentler, more sensitive, and less subject to the vices that follow
from egotism and hard hearts, do not really possess a sense of justice; that they obey their feelings rather than their consciences.
This observation is truer but it proves nothing. It is not nature but
rather education and social conditions that cause this difference.
Neither the one nor the other has accustomed women to the idea
of what is just, only to the idea of what is becoming or proper. Removed from public affairs, from everything that is decided according to the most rigorous idea of justice, or according to positive
laws, they concern themselves with and act upon precisely those

things which are regulated by natural propriety and by feeling. It is therefore unjust to advance as grounds for continuing to refuse women the enjoyment of their natural rights those reasons that only have some kind of reality because women do not enjoy these rights in the first place.

If one admits such arguments against women, it would also be necessary to take away the rights of citizenship from that portion of the people who, having to work without respite, can neither acquire enlightenment nor exercise its reason, and soon little by little the only men who would be permitted to be citizens would be those who had followed a course in public law.

. . . It is natural for a woman to nurse her children, to care for them in their infancy; attached to her home by these cares, weaker than a man, it is also natural that she lead a more retiring, more domestic life. Women would therefore be in the same class with men who are obliged by their station or profession to work several hours a day. This may be a reason for not preferring them in elections, but it cannot be the grounds for their legal exclusion.

. . . I demand now that these arguments be refuted by other means than pleasantries or ranting; above all that someone show me a natural difference between men and women that can legitimately found [women's] exclusion from a right.

Lynn Hunt, ed., *The French Revolution and Human Rights: A Brief Documentary History*. Boston: St. Martin's Press, 1996, pp. 119–21.

## Document 15: The King Condemns the Revolution

*The king's attempted escape from France on June 20, 1791, marked the fateful turning point in relations between the royal family and the French people. Louis left behind the following proclamation. Meant as a rationale for his flight, it revealed his true attitude toward the Revolution and the new government, which he called vicious and barbarous. More than anything else, it discredited him in the eyes of both revolutionary leaders and the people.*

While the King could hope to see order and wellbeing restored by the means employed by the National Assembly, and by his residence near that Assembly, no sacrifice was too great for him; he even accepted loss of liberty, of which he had been deprived since the month of October 1789. But today, when the outcome of all his efforts is to see royalty destroyed, property violated, personal security in jeopardy, complete anarchy in every part of the Empire, without any semblance of an authority sufficient to stop it, the King, having protested against all the acts issued in his name during his captivity, believes it his duty to put Frenchmen in possession of an account of his conduct.

In July 1789, the King, confident in his conscience, did not fear to come among Parisians. . . . Everyone is aware how crimes committed then went unpunished. The King, yielding to the wish expressed by the army of Parisians established himself with his family in the Tuileries. Nothing was ready for his reception, and the King, far from finding the conveniences to which he was accustomed in his other establishments, did not even find the amenities which persons in easy circumstances enjoy. In spite of every constraint, he believed it his duty, the very day after his arrival, to reassure the provinces concerning his stay in Paris.

A more painful sacrifice was in store for him: he was to be separated from his bodyguards, whose loyalty he had proved. Two were massacred, several were wounded carrying out the order they had received not to open fire. . . . The guarding of the King was entrusted to soldiers of the French Guards and to the Parisian National Guard, under orders of the municipality of Paris, to which the commanding officer was responsible.

The King was thus seen to be a prisoner in his own estates, for what else could one be called who was forcibly surrounded by people suspect to him? It is not to indict the National Guard that I recall these details, but to report the exact truth; on the contrary, I acknowledge its loyalty until it was misled by sedition-mongers.

The King ordered the convocation of the Estates General and granted double representation to the Third Estate. The mingling of orders, the sacrifices of 23 June, all that was his work; but his solicitude has been misconstrued and misrepresented. At the time when the Estates General called itself the National Assembly, one calls to mind the intrigues of the seditious in several provinces: one recalls the agitations which were raised to circumvent the clauses in the *cahiers* which provided that the making of the laws should be carried out in concert with the King. The Assembly put the King outside of the Constitution by refusing him the right to sanction constitutional acts, and classifying in that way whatever it pleased it to so classify, and by limiting his veto [over purely legislative acts], to a suspension [until] the third legislature. He was granted 25,000,000 [*livres*] which were completely absorbed in the expenses necessitated by the lustre essential to his household. He was left the usufruct [right to use] of several domains with constricting requirements, so depriving him of the patrimony of his ancestors; . . .

Should the different aspects of administration be examined, it will be seen that the King has been brushed aside: he has no part in making laws. He can only request the Assembly to interest itself in such or such a matter. As for the administration of justice, he can only expedite the provision of judges and name the King's commissaries whose duties are much less considerable than those of the former *procureurs-généraux*. The public part [of the work] has devolved on new officers. There remained one last prerogative, the finest of all, that of reprieve and the commutation of penalties. You have taken it from the King. Now juries exercise it, applying the meaning of the law according to their will. That [provision] diminishes the King's royal majesty [for] people were accustomed to have recourse to him as to a common centre of goodness and beneficence.

Internal administration in the departments is inconvenienced by officiousness which hinders the working of the machinery; ministerial surveillance is reduced to a sham. The Societies of Friends of the Constitution [*i.e., Jacobins*] are more powerful [than the government] and nullify [its] actions.

The King has been declared supreme commander of the army, but all the work has been done by committees of the National Assembly without his assistance. The King was granted the right of nomination to several positions, but again he was contraverted in his choices; selections for general-officers in the army had to be reviewed because they displeased the clubs; it is to them alone that most of the revolts in the regiments must be attributed. When the army no longer respects its officers it becomes the terror and scourge of the State. The King has always held that officers must be punished in the same way as soldiers and that the door must be open for the latter to be promoted according to merit.

In foreign affairs, the King has been granted the right to nominate ambassadors and conduct negotiations. The right to wage war has been taken from him, but it should not be thought that he declared it without consideration. The right to make peace is of another kind altogether. The King would only want to make the one with the nation's support, but what power will want to enter negotiations when the right of revision is granted to the National Assembly? Apart from the necessary secrecy, which it is impossible to keep in an assembly which must deliberate in public, they like to treat only with the person who can, without any hindrance, agree to the contract.

In the realm of finance, the King recognized, before the meeting of the Estates General, the nation's right to grant taxes, and in this respect, on 23 June, he granted all that had been sought. On 4

February [1790] the King urged the Assembly to take up the question of the finances; it did so only later. There is as yet no exact statement of receipts and expenditure but hypothetical calculations have been accepted. Ordinary taxation is in arrears and the expedient of 1,200,000,000 *assignats* is almost exhausted. In this respect, the King has been left only unproductive appointments [to make]. He understands the difficulties of administration in this field, and if the machinery could work without his direct supervision, His Majesty's only regret would be in not reducing the imposts, something which he wished to do and would have done but for the American War.

The King has been declared supreme head of the administration of the Kingdom, but he can change nothing without the Assembly's decision. The leaders of the dominant party have so distrusted the King's agents, and the penalties imposed on unjust officers have aroused so much uneasiness, that those agents have remained powerless.

This form of government is vicious for two main reasons: the Assembly exceeds the limits of its power and involves itself in justice and internal administration; and through its Committee on Investigations it exercises the most barbarous of all despotisms. Associations have been established, known by the name of Friends of the Constitution, which constitute corporations infinitely more dangerous than those which formerly existed. They deliberate on every aspect of government and exercise such a preponderance that all bodies, not even excepting the National Assembly, act only by their command. The King does not think it possible to preserve such a form of government. The nearer the end of the Assembly's labours approaches, the more wise men lose their influence. New regulations, instead of applying balm to old wounds, aggravate discontents. The thousands of journals and scurrilous pamphlets, which only echo the clubs, perpetuate disorder, and the Assembly has never dared to remedy the situation; the tendency is towards a metaphysical government impossible to operate.

Frenchmen, is that why you elected your representatives? Do you want the despotism of the clubs to supersede the monarchy under which the Kingdom has prospered for fourteen hundred years? The love of Frenchmen for their King is counted among their virtues. I have had signs of this too touching to be forgotten. . . .

It is natural, after all these provocations, and [given] the impossibility of the King preventing evil, that he should have sought to ensure his own safety.

Frenchmen, and especially you inhabitants of the good city of Paris, distrust the suggestions of sedition-mongers and return to your King. He will always be your friend, [and especially] when your holy religion is respected, when government is on a stable footing and liberty established on unshakable foundations.

Signed, Louis.

Paris, 20 June 1791.

P.S. The King forbids his ministers to sign any order in his name until they have received further instructions, and he enjoins the Keeper of the Seal to send him the Seal when so required.

Signed, Louis.

D.I. Wright, ed., *The French Revolution: Introductory Documents*. St. Lucia: University of Queensland Press, 1974, pp. 91–95.

## Document 16: An Englishman Calls for Abandoning the Monarchy

*After the king's unsuccessful and, to many, traitorous escape attempt, those revolutionary leaders who favored a republic found their cause strengthened. On July 1, 1791, the following letter was posted on the door of the Assembly's meeting hall. It was drafted by Thomas Paine, the English-born writer whose radical work,* Common Sense, *had played a crucial role in the American Revolution. Paine had become a French citizen in 1792 and was a supporter of the ongoing French Revolution; here he suggests that monarchy in any form, even that of constitutional monarchy, is wrongheaded and dangerous, implying that a republic is the only viable alternative.*

Brethren and Fellow Citizens:

The serene tranquillity, the mutual confidence which prevailed amongst us, during the time of the late King's escape, the indifference with which we beheld him return, are unequivocal proofs that the absence of a King is more desirable than his presence, and that he is not only a political superfluity, but a grievous burden, pressing hard on the whole nation.

Let us not be imposed on by sophisms [invalid arguments]; all that concerns this is reduced to four points.

He has abdicated the throne in having fled from his post. Abdication and desertion are not characterized by the length of absence; but by the single act of flight. In the present instance, the act is everything, and the time nothing.

The nation can never give back its confidence to a man who, false to his trust, perjured to his oath, conspires a clandestine flight, obtains a fraudulent passport, conceals a King of France under the disguise of a valet, directs his course towards a frontier covered with traitors and deserters, and evidently meditates a return into our country, with a force capable of imposing his own despotic laws.

Should his flight be considered as his own act, or the act of those who fled with him? Was it a spontaneous resolution of his own, or was it inspired by others? The alternative is immaterial; whether fool or hypocrite, idiot or traitor, he has proved himself equally unworthy of the important functions that had been delegated to him.

In every sense in which the question can be considered, the reciprocal obligation which subsisted between us is dissolved. He holds no longer any authority. We owe him no longer obedience. We see in him no more than an indifferent person; we can regard him only as Louis Capet.

The history of France presents little else than a long series of public calamity, which takes its source from the vices of Kings; we have been the wretched victims that have never ceased to suffer either for them or by them. The catalogue of their oppressions was complete, but to complete the sum of their crimes, treason was yet wanting. Now the only vacancy is filled up, the dreadful list is full; the system is exhausted; there are no remaining errors for them to commit; their reign is consequently at an end.

What kind of office must that be in a government which requires for its execution neither experience nor ability, that may be abandoned to the desperate chance of birth, that may be filled by an idiot, a madman, a tyrant, with equal effect as by the good, the virtuous, and the wise? An office of this nature is a mere nonentity; it is a place of show, not of use. Let France, then, arrived at the age of reason, no longer be deluded by the sound of words, and let her deliberately examine, if a King, however insignificant and contemptible in himself, may not at the same time be extremely dangerous.

The thirty millions which it costs to support a King in the eclat of stupid brutal luxury, presents us with an easy method of reducing taxes, which reduction would at once relieve the people, and stop the progress of political corruption. The grandeur of nations consists, not, as Kings pretend, in the splendour of thrones, but in a conspicuous sense of their own dignity, and in a just disdain of those barbarous follies and crimes which, under the sanction of Royalty, have hitherto desolated Europe.

As to the personal safety of Louis Capet, it is so much the more confirmed, as France will not stoop to degrade herself by a spirit of revenge against a wretch who has dishonoured himself. In defending a just and glorious cause, it is not possible to degrade it, and the universal tranquillity which prevails is an undeniable proof that a free people know how to respect themselves.

John H. Stewart, ed., *A Documentary Survey of the French Revolution*. New York: Macmillan, 1951, pp. 215–16.

## Document 17: The Guillotine: More Humane?

*Following is an excerpt from the report submitted to the Assembly on March 7, 1792, by Dr. Louis, secretary of the French Academy of Surgery, who had been asked to recommend a method of execution more humane than the traditional headsman's ax or sword. Louis suggested the device that was at first called the Louisette, after himself, but that later became known as the guillotine, after another advocate of its use, physician Joseph-Ignace Guillotin.*

The Committee on Legislation has done me the honor of consulting me concerning two letters written by the National Assembly with regard to the execution of Title I, article 3 of the Penal Code, providing that *every one condemned* to the penalty of death *shall be decapitated.* In these letters the Minister of Justice and the directory of the Department of Paris, on the basis of representations made to them, consider it urgently necessary to determine exactly the manner of procedure in the execution of the law, lest, through defective means or by lack of experience and skill, capital punishment become horrible for the victim and the spectators. . . .

I consider the representations just and the fears well founded. Experience and reason alike indicate that the method hitherto used in decapitating criminals exposes them to a capital punishment more frightful than mere deprivation of life, which is the formal aim of the law; in order to achieve it, the execution must be made instantly and by a single blow; examples give proof of the difficulty of succeeding therein.

The decapitation of M. de Lally [an execution that took place in 1766] must here be recalled; he was on his knees, his eyes bandaged; the executioner struck him on the nape of the neck; the blow did not sever the head . . . ; the body . . . was turned over; and it was only with three or four blows of the sword that the head was finally separated from the body. This butchery was viewed with horror. . . .

In Germany the executioners are more experienced as a result of the frequency of this method of execution, chiefly because women, whatever their status, are subject to no other type of execution; perfect execution, however, often fails, in spite of the precaution, in certain places, of fastening the victim in an armchair.

In Denmark there are two positions and two instruments for decapitation. The execution which might be called *honorable* is performed with a sword. The criminal, on his knees, has a bandage over his eyes, and his hands are free. If the punishment is to be ignominious, the victim is bound, laid on his stomach, and decapitated with an axe.

No one is ignorant of the fact that cutting instruments have little or no effect when they strike perpendicularly; by examining them under a microscope it may be seen that they are only more or less fine saws, which must be operated by sliding over the body which is to be divided. One would not succeed in decapitating by a single blow with an axe or knife, the edge of which was in a straight line; but with a convex blade, as on old battle-axes, the blow struck acts perpendicularly only at the middle part of the circle; but the instrument, in penetrating the continuity of the parts it divides, has an oblique sliding action on the sides, and effectively achieves its end.

In considering the structure of the neck, the center of which is the vertebral column composed of several bones, the connection of which forms overlappings so that there is no joint, it is impossible to be assured of a prompt and perfect separation by trusting to an agent whose skill is influenced by moral and physical factors; for certainty one must depend on invariable mechanical means, the force and effect of which may likewise be determined. That is the course followed in England: the body of the criminal is laid face down between two posts connected at the top by a crosspiece, from which the convex axe is dropped on the neck by means of a release. The back of the instrument must be strong and heavy enough to act effectively, like a pile driver; it is known that its force increases in proportion to the height from which it falls.

It would be easy to construct a similar machine, the performance of which would be unfailing. Decapitation would be performed instantly, according to the spirit and aim of the new law. It would be easy to test it on corpses, and even on live sheep.

John H. Stewart, ed., *A Documentary Survey of the French Revolution*. New York: Macmillan, 1951, pp. 344–45.

## Document 18: The Decree of Divorce

*The lengthy divorce decree passed by the Assembly on September 20, 1792, reflected the secularizing influence of the Revolution, part of its removal of various aspects of private life from church control. As these excerpts prove, even by today's standards these were liberal and enlightened divorce laws.*

The National Assembly, considering the importance of enabling Frenchmen to enjoy the privilege of divorce, a consequence of individual liberty, which would be doomed by indissoluble engagements; considering that already a number of married couples have not waited, in order to enjoy the advantages of the constitutional provision according to which marriage is only a civil contract, until the law had regulated the manner and consequences of divorce, decrees as follows.

## I
## Grounds for Divorce

1. Marriage may be dissolved by divorce.
2. Divorce shall take place by mutual consent of husband and wife.
3. One of the parties may have divorce pronounced on the mere allegation of incompatibility of disposition or character.
4. Each of the parties likewise may have divorce pronounced on certain determined grounds, to wit: 1st, the insanity, madness, or violence of one of the parties; 2nd, the sentence of one of them to corporal or ignominious punishments; 3rd, crimes, cruelty, or serious injuries on the part of one against the other; 4th, notoriously dissolute morals; 5th, the desertion of the wife by the husband or of the husband by the wife for at least two years; 6th, the absence of one of them, without news, for at least five years; 7th, emigration, in the cases anticipated by law, particularly by the decree of 8 April, 1792.
5. Married people now separated by a judgment executed, or in the last resort, shall have mutual right to have divorce pronounced.
6. All requests and suits for separation not granted are dismissed and abolished; each of the parties shall pay his (or her) expenses. Judgments of separation not executed, or impugned by appeal ... remain as void, reserving to parties the right to have recourse to means of divorce according to the terms of the present law.
7. Henceforth, no separation may be pronounced; married parties may be disunited only by divorce.

## II
## Divorce Procedures
### Divorce by Mutual Consent

1. The husband and wife who conjointly request divorce shall be required to convoke an assembly of at least six of the nearest

relatives, or friends in default of relatives; three of the relatives or friends shall be chosen by the husband, the other three by the wife.

2. The assembly shall be convoked on an appointed day and at the place agreed upon with the relatives or friends; there shall be at least one month's interval between the day of the convocation and that of the assembly. A clerk shall serve the instrument of convocation upon the relatives or friends who are summoned.

3. If, on the day of convocation, one or more of the relatives or friends who are summoned cannot attend the assembly, the married parties shall have them replaced by other relatives or friends.

4. The two married parties shall present themselves in person at the assembly; there they shall state that they are seeking a divorce. The relatives or friends assembled shall make such observations and representations as they deem suitable. If the married parties persist in their intention, a municipal official, summoned for such purpose, shall draw up an instrument stating merely that the relatives or friends have heard the married parties in a duly convoked assembly, and that they have been unable to reconcile them. The draft of such instrument, signed by the members of the assembly, the two married parties, and the municipal official, with mention of those who did not know how or were unable to sign, shall be deposited with the clerk of the municipality; a copy thereof shall be delivered to the married parties gratis and without registration fee.

5. One month at the least and six months at the most after the date of the instrument designated in the preceding article, the married parties may present themselves before the public official who is responsible for recording marriages in the municipality where the husband is domiciled; and, at their request, the said public official shall be required to pronounce their divorce, without taking cognizance of grounds. The parties and the public official shall comply with the forms prescribed on this matter in the law concerning records of births, deaths, and marriages.

6. After the interval of six months mentioned in the preceding article, the married parties may be admitted to divorce by mutual consent merely by observing again the same formalities and the same intervals of time.

7. In case of the minority of the married parties, or of one of them, or if they have children born of their marriage, the intervals above indicated, of one month for the convocation of the fam-

ily assembly, and of at least one month after the instrument of nonconciliation, in order to obtain divorce, shall be doubled; but the irrevocable interval of six months after the instrument of nonconciliation, in order to obtain divorce shall remain the same.

John H. Stewart, ed., *A Documentary Survey of the French Revolution*. New York: Macmillan, 1951, pp. 333–35.

## Document 19: The King Indicted

*Following are a few of the thirty-three articles of indictment brought against Louis XVI on December 11, 1792, only six weeks before his conviction and execution.*

Louis, the French people accuses you of having committed a multitude of crimes in order to establish your tyranny by destroying its liberty.

1. On 20 June, 1789, you attacked the sovereignty of the people by suspending the assemblies of its representatives and by driving them by violence from the place of their sessions. . . .
2. On 23 June you wished to dictate laws to the nation; you surrounded its representatives with troops; you presented them with two royal declarations, subversive of every liberty, and you ordered them to separate. Your declarations and the minutes of the Assembly establish these outrages undeniably.
3. You caused an army to march against the citizens of Paris; your satellites caused their blood to flow, and you withdrew this army only when the capture of the Bastille and the general insurrection apprised you that the people were victorious. . . .
6. For a long time you contemplated flight: on 23 February a memoir was sent to you indicating the means therefor, and you approved it. On the 28th a multitude of nobles and officers distributed themselves throughout your apartments at the Tuileries Palace to facilitate such flight. . . . On 21 June you made your escape with a false passport; you left a declaration against those same constitutional articles. . . .
7. After your arrest at Varennes, the exercise of the executive power was for a time taken from your hands; and still you conspired. . . . On 14 September you apparently accepted the Constitution; your speeches announced a desire to maintain it, and you worked to overthrow it before it even was achieved. . . .
15. Your brothers, enemies of the state, have rallied the *émigrés* under their colors; they have raised regiments, borrowed money, and contracted alliances in your name; you disavowed

them only when you were quite certain that you could not harm their plans.

John H. Stewart, ed., *A Documentary Survey of the French Revolution*. New York: Macmillan, 1951, pp. 386–89.

## Document 20: The New Copyright Law

*This well-considered and comprehensive set of regulations protecting the works of authors and artists, passed on July 19, 1793, was one of numerous pieces of progressive legislation enacted by the government between late 1792 and mid-1794. Others included, to name only a few, the establishment of a revolutionary calendar, the abolition of black slavery in French colonies, and rules regulating the postal service, education, and public charity and relief.*

1. Authors of writings of every sort, composers of music, and painters and draftsmen who have pictures or drawings engraved shall enjoy, throughout their entire life, the exclusive right to sell, to have sold, or to distribute their works in the territory of the Republic, and to assign the ownership thereof in whole or in part.
2. Their heirs or assignees shall enjoy the same right during the period of ten years after the death of the authors.
3. On the requisition and for the benefit of the authors, composers, painters or draftsmen and others, their heirs or assignees, the peace officers shall be required to have confiscated all copies of editions which have been printed or engraved without the formal and written permission of the authors.
4. Any infringer shall be required to pay the real owner an amount equal to the price of 3,000 copies of the original edition.
5. Any retailer of a pirated edition, if he is not identified as the infringer, shall be required to pay the real owner an amount equal to the price of 500 copies of the original edition.
6. Any citizen who publishes a work, either of literature or engraving, of any type whatsoever, shall be obliged to deposit two copies thereof in the *Bibliothèque Nationale* [National Library] or the Bureau of Engraving of the Republic, where he shall receive a receipt signed by the librarian, without which he may have no recourse to law for the prosecution of infringers.
7. The heirs of an author of a work of literature or engraving, or of any other product of the mind or genius which belongs to the fine arts, shall have exclusive proprietary rights thereto for ten years.

John H. Stewart, ed., *A Documentary Survey of the French Revolution*. New York: Macmillan, 1951, p. 515.

## Document 21: The Queen Faces Death

*This letter, penned by Marie-Antoinette in the early morning of October 16, 1793, the day of her execution by the revolutionary tribunal, was addressed to Louis's sister, Madame Elisabeth. Whatever her shortcomings as a ruler, the queen must be credited with facing a cruel and brutal death with courage and dignity.*

This 16 October, half-past four in the morning. It is to you, my sister, that I write for the last time. I have just been condemned not to a shameful death, it is such only for criminals, but to go and join your brother. Innocent like him, I hope to show the same steadfastness as he in these last moments. I am calm, as one is when one's conscience reproaches one with nothing; I deeply regret leaving my poor children; you know that I lived only for them, and you, my good, loving sister, you who have by your friendship sacrificed everything to be with us, what a position I leave you in!

I learnt during the proceedings of the trial that my daughter has been separated from you. Alas! the poor child. I dare not write to her, my letter would not reach her, and I do not even know whether this will reach you, receive for them both my blessing here. I hope that one day, when they are older, they will be able to join you and enjoy all your loving care. May they both think of those notions that I have always tried to instill in them: that principles and the exact execution of their duties are the very basis of life; that their friendship and mutual trust will bring them happiness. May my daughter realize that, given her age, she must always assist her brother with the good counsel that her [this word has been erased in the original] her greater experience and her friendship may inspire in him; may my son, in turn, give his sister all the care and service that friendship may inspire; lastly, may they both feel that, in whatever position they find themselves, they will be truly happy only by being united. May they follow our example: how often, in our misfortunes, our friendship has given us consolation, while, in better times, we have been able to enjoy our happiness twofold by sharing it with a friend; and where can one find dearer, more loving care than in one's own family?

May my son never forget his father's last words, which I repeat to him now: let him never seek to avenge our death. I have to say one thing that is very painful to my heart. I know how much that child must have caused you pain [the authorities had forced the boy to make damaging and mostly false accusations against his mother and aunt]; forgive him, my dear sister; think of his age and how easy it is to make a child say whatever one wishes, and even things that he does not understand; the day will come, I hope, when he will feel all the more the value of your care and your kindness to us both.

It remains to me to entrust my last thoughts to you. I would like to have written them down at the beginning of the trial, but, apart from the fact that I was not allowed to write, everything moved with such rapidity, that I really did not have the time. I die in the Roman, Catholic, apostolic religion in which I was brought up and which I have always professed, expecting no spiritual consolation, not knowing whether there are still priests of that religion here, but, given where I am, it would no doubt expose them too much if they tried to come here. I sincerely ask forgiveness of God for all the sins that I may have committed in my life. I hope that, in his goodness, he will accept my last wishes, together with those that I made long since, that he may receive my soul in his mercy and goodness. I ask pardon of all those I have known and of you, my sister, in particular, for all the trouble that, without wishing it, I may have caused you. I pardon all my enemies the ill that they have done me. I say farewell to my aunts and [a word is erased] and to all my brothers and sisters. The idea of being separated from my friends for ever and the sorrow this will cause them are a source of bitter regret that I take with me as I die. May they know at least that, up to my last moment, I thought of them.

Farewell, my good and loving sister; may this letter reach you safely! Think always of me, I embrace you with all my heart, as well as my poor, dear children: my God! How dreadful it is to leave them for ever! Farewell! Farewell! I have now only my spiritual duties to concern myself with. Since I am not free in my actions, I may not be allowed a priest, but I declare here that I will not say a word to him and shall treat him as a perfect stranger.

Marie-Antoinette.

Olivier Blanc, *Last Letters: Prisons and Prisoners of the French Revolution, 1793–1794.* Translated by Alan Sheridan. New York: Farrar, Straus & Giroux, 1987, pp. 126–27.

## Document 22: The Committee of Public Safety Dominates the Government

*This eyewitness account of the manner in which the main organ of the Terror, the Committee of Public Safety, intimidated into submission the more numerous moderates in the government in 1794, comes from the memoirs of Antoine-Claire Thibaudeau, who served for a time as president of the National Convention.*

The National Convention itself was now only nominally a representative body, having become a passive instrument of the Terror. Upon the ruins of its independence rose the monstrous dictatorship of the famous committee of public safety. The Terror isolated and stupefied the representatives as much as it did the ordinary citizens. A member came to the Assembly with misgivings, heedful of his words and actions lest they be made into a crime. In fact, one had to be careful of everything, the place where one sat, one's gestures, murmurs, smiles. The summit of the Mountain being accounted the place of the highest republicanism, all edged in that direction. The Right had been deserted after the expulsion of the Girondins. Either through conscientious scruples or from shame, their companions refused to join the Mountain and took refuge with the Plain [the group of deputies in the National Convention who followed a centrist, noncommital line]. The Plain was always ready to receive those who desired the safety of its complacency and negativeness. The more pusillanimous [timid] refused to identify themselves with any group and would change from seat to seat, thinking that they would thus outwit the spies and give themselves a mixed complexion which would offend no one. The most prudent of all did better still. Fearing to be contaminated and especially to be compromised, they never sat down at all. They remained at the foot of the tribune away from the circle of benches. On turbulent occasions when there was danger in voting against the propositions repugnant to them, they slipped furtively out of the hall.

The majority of the Convention did not want the Terror any more than did the majority of the nation. . . . But through weakness or fear, it showed no open disapproval of what it privately censured, and preserved a mournful silence. The sessions, previously so long and stormy, were now for the most part calm and formal, lasting only an hour or so. What little liberty they had was in regard to things of no importance. The more serious matters they left to the committee of public safety, and acted according to its wishes. Members of the committee or its reporter would keep them waiting as one waits for sovereign powers and heads of states. When members of the committee came to the hall where the sittings were being held, vile courtiers advanced in front of them as if they were announcing the masters of the world. Faces were scrutinized to see whether they were bringing a decree of proscription or the news of a victory. The reporter mounted the tribune amid profound silence, and if any spoke after he had left the floor, it was only to emphasize what he had said. His conclusions were always tacitly adopted without a formal vote. When the triumphs of the armies were announced, his insolent attitude seemed to declare, "It is not you, or the army, or the people that are victorious; it is the committee of public safety." And they had, in fact, taken over all power of legislation and government in both planning and execution. They finally took the power of proscription away from the committee of general security, leaving to it the doubtful privilege of making out the lists.

E.L. Higgins, ed., *The French Revolution as Told by Contemporaries.* Boston: Houghton Mifflin, 1939, pp. 314–15.

## Document 23: The Last Words of a Victim of the Terror

*In April 1794, at the height of the Terror, Louis-Henri-Marthe, marquis de Gouy D'Arsy, a distinguished military officer and former Assembly deputy, went to the guillotine for suspicion of disloyalty to the Revolution. His magnificently phrased and highly moving last letter, addressed to his wife, captures not only the cruelty and injustice that characterized this stage of the Revolution and the desire of reasonable Frenchmen to return to the mood of rationality and civility in which the Revolution had begun, but also the transcendent power of love in the face of certain death.*

So what remains for me to do. . . . Ah! My friend, the most painful of acts. . . . It remains to me to leave you! Here I admit, to the shame of human weakness, but to the glory of my heart, that all my physical strength deserts me. My moral faculties are destroyed, tears flood my face; and because I feel so much, it seems to me that I have ceased to be, before suffering death. This state of nothingness and pain is horrible; the yearnings I feel are frightful. . . . To leave my family, to be separated for ever from my dear companion, to be far away from my dear children, to abandon all that in the flower of my age, without accident, without glory, without disease, to be in full possession of my faculties to appreciate what I am losing, all my affections to know what I am leaving, all my senses to struggle against the mortal stroke that is to separate me from the living, all that, my dear, is more than I can bear and is killing me in advance; so conjugal love, which has brought me so much delight, now causes all my pain! Thus fatherhood, which has brought me so many sweet moments, now gives me so many regrets! And one cannot leave it! And yet, in a few moments, I shall be in another world!

Ah! My God, where shall I find the strength to undertake such a journey. Without friends, with no one to console me, isolated from all that I love, I feel around me nothing but prison, judges and executioners! But my conscience sustains me, my innocence consoles me, pity comforts me and God calls me: it is on his paternal bosom that I shall throw myself. . . .

Do not pity me, my friend, in a few hours I shall be happier than you; your ills alone torment me, they will be excessive, I see from here your pain, I sense your tears flowing. . . .

Ah! How sweet it would be to wipe them away, to embrace you again, to hold my children in my arms once more. . . . But no. . . .

Farewell, all my beloved children! Farewell, my dear Baptiste, my beloved; I die your friend, your husband, your lover; I excuse my judges, I forgive my executioners, I wish every happiness to our country: I shall not cease to say so, for your consolation, for your happiness and that of our children.

Farewell! Farewell! You who were everything for me in this world, and whom I shall never forget in the next, farewell, for a time; that hope sweetens this cruel moment for me. . . . Farewell, dearest half of myself; we must make an end; farewell! I tear myself from your arms, I throw myself into God's bosom; come and join me there one day, with all our children. The others await me, farewell! Receive my last kiss, it is loving, pure, it is the price of the great courage of which you have given me such honourable proof, so worthy of the esteem of my loved ones!

My body perishes, my soul flies up, my heart will not leave you. . . .

I enclose a few letters; those from my children, for example, from my mother, my sister, which I managed to hide from the searches of the investigators sent into the prison by our tyrants, our executioners. . . . Plus my hair, which I cut off myself; I didn't want it to reach you sullied by the hands of Robespierre's executioner. Farewell again, a hundred kisses for each of our children! A hundred kisses for my father and mother! A thousand for you, my friend! To my eldest son I send the key to my little case; I have wrapped it in paper, which contains a few important words for him and his brothers; you will give to all the others some other object that belonged to me and which may prove to them that I love them all equally. Let them copy out this letter and you, my dear, keep the original, for it concerns you. Can I write anything without your beloved name finding itself naturally on the paper! It is in my heart, on my lips and everywhere. Farewell, yet again: how heartrending that word would be were I not sure that you would do everything in your power to join me one day: our little ones await us; already, I hear them calling me; the others will join us later; take care to bring them up well. Ah! My friend! My beloved friend! How I owe you everything that I have demanded of you in the name of the bitter sacrifice of all my joys, all the happiness and all the compensation that perhaps I was worthy of tasting after so many ills!

What a sin it is to murder a citizen thus! But . . . what am I saying? I promised to endure my sacrifice without complaint and I am already forgetting my oath.

Ah, my God! Forgive mankind, surrounded by weakness and woe. And you, my dear wife, be comforted; I summon up all my courage to offer you the homage of all that remains of my virtue: farewell, receive my last kiss. . . . My body perishes, my soul flies up, my heart does not leave you. . . . It could never leave you. . . . O my country! . . . My country! May you soon be delivered at last from the bloody executioners who wish to dishonour you before all nations!

Olivier Blanc, *Last Letters: Prisons and Prisoners of the French Revolution, 1793–1794.* Translated by Alan Sheridan. New York: Farrar, Straus & Giroux, 1987, pp. 205–207.

## Document 24: Robespierre's Swan Song

*This powerful speech, given to the Convention by Robespierre on July 26, 1794, in response to charges brought against him by the moderates, turned out to be his last public pronouncement. His lofty protestations that he was merely a defender of freedom and virtue and a victim of evil forces trying to destroy the government fell on deaf ears; he was arrested the next day and on July 28 died on the same guillotine that had dispatched so many of his opponents.*

When I see the mass of vices the torrent of the Revolution has rolled pell-mell with the civic virtues, I have sometimes trembled for fear of becoming tainted in the eyes of posterity by the impure vicinage of those perverse men who mingled in the ranks of the sincere defenders of humanity; but the overthrow of the rival factions has, as it were, emancipated all the vices; they believed that the only question for them was to make division of the country as a booty rather than make her free and prosperous. I am thankful that the fury that animates them against everything that opposes itself to their projects has traced the line of demarcation between them and all right-minded people; but if the Verres and the Catilines [famous traitors to the government of the ancient Roman Republic] of France believe themselves already far enough advanced in the career of crime to expose on the rostrum the head of their accuser, I also have but now promised to my fellow citizens a testament formidable to the oppressors of the people, and I bequeath to them from this moment opprobrium [public disgrace] and death! . . .

Frenchmen, do not allow your enemies to degrade your souls and to unnerve your virtues by a baleful heresy! . . . Citizens, efface from the tombstones this impious maxim which throws a funeral crape upon all nature and flings insults upon death. Rather engrave that: "Death is the beginning of immortality!" My people, remember that if in the republic justice does not reign with absolute sway, and if this word does not signify love of equality and of country, then liberty is but a vain phrase! O people, you who are feared—whom one flatters! you who are despised; you who are acknowledged sovereign, and are ever being treated as a slave— remember that wherever justice does not reign, it is the passions of the magistrates that reign instead, and that the people have changed their chains and not their destinies!

Remember that there exists in your bosom a league of knaves struggling against public virtue, and that it has a greater influence than yourselves upon your own affairs—a league that dreads you and flatters you in the mass, but proscribes you in detail in the person of all good citizens! . . .

Know, then, that any man who will rise to defend public right and public morals will be overwhelmed with outrage and proscribed by the knaves! Know, also, that every friend of liberty will ever be placed between duty and calumny; that those who cannot be accused of treason will be accused of ambition; that the influence of uprightness and principles will be compared to tyranny and the violence of factions; that your confidence and your esteem will become certificates of proscription for all your friends; that the cries of oppressed patriotism will be called cries of sedition; and that, as they do not dare to attack you in mass, you will be proscribed in detail in the person of all good citizens, until the ambitious shall have organized their tyranny. Such is the empire of the tyrants armed against us! Such is the influence of their league with corrupt men, ever inclined to serve them.

Thus the unprincipled wretches impose upon us law to force us to betray the people, under penalty of being called dictators! Shall we subscribe to this law? No! Let us defend the people at the risk of becoming their victims! Let them hasten to the scaffold by the path of crime and we by that of virtue. Shall we say that all is well? Shall we continue to praise by force of habit or practice that which is wrong? We would ruin the country. Shall we reveal hidden abuses? Shall we denounce traitors? We shall be told that we are unsettling the constituted authorities, that we are endeavoring to acquire personal influence at their cost. What are we to do? Our duty! What objection can be made to him who wishes to tell the truth and who consents to die for it? Let us then say that there exists a conspiracy against public liberty; that it owes its strength to a criminal coalition that is intriguing even in the bosom of the Convention; that this coalition has accomplices in the Committee of General Safety and in the offices of this committee, which they control; that the enemies of the republic have opposed this committee to the Committee of Public Safety and have thus constituted two governments; that members of the Committee of Public Safety have entered into this scheme of mischief; that the coalition thus formed tries to ruin all patriots and the fatherland.

What is the remedy for this evil? Punish the traitors, renew the offices of the Committee of General Safety, weed out this committee itself, and subordinate it to the Committee of Public Safety; weed out the Committee of Public Safety also, constitute the unity of the government under the supreme authority of the National Convention, which is the center and the judge, and thus crush all factions by the weight of national authority, in order to erect upon their ruins the power of justice and of liberty. Such are my principles. If it be impossible to support them without being taken for an ambitious one, I shall conclude that principles are proscribed and that tyranny reigns among us, but not that I should remain silent! For what can be objected to a man who is in the right and knows how to die for his country?

I was created to battle against crime, not to govern it. The time has not come when upright men may serve their country with impunity! The defenders of liberty will be but outlaws so long as a horde of knaves shall rule!

William Safire, ed., *Lend Me Your Ears: Great Speeches in History*. New York: W.W. Norton, 1997, pp. 382–84.

## Document 25: Napoléon Takes Charge

*In this public statement of November 10, 1799, his first after becoming the nation's First Consul, Napoléon used the kind of propaganda typical of historical dictators, who have so often, in seizing power, claimed to be rescuing the government from traitors and rebels and restoring order at the request of reasonable leaders and, of course, for the good of the people.*

On my return to Paris I found division among all authorities, and agreement upon only one point, namely, that the Constitution was half destroyed and was unable to save liberty.

All parties came to me, confided to me their designs, disclosed their secrets, and requested my support; I refused to be the man of a party.

The Council of Elders summoned me; I answered its appeal. A plan of general restoration had been devised by men whom the nation has been accustomed to regard as the defenders of liberty, equality, and property; this plan required an examination, calm, free, exempt from all influence and all fear. Accordingly, the Council of Elders resolved upon the removal of the Legislative Body. . . . It gave me the responsibility of disposing the force necessary for its independence. I believed it my duty to my fellow citizens, to the soldiers perishing in our armies, to the national glory acquired at the cost of their blood, to accept the command.

The Councils assembled. . . . Republican troops guaranteed their security from without, but assassins created terror within. Several deputies of the Council of Five Hundred, armed with stilettos [knives] and firearms, circulated threats of death around them.

The plans which ought to have been developed were withheld, the majority disorganized, the boldest orators disconcerted, and the futility of every wise proposition was evident. . . .

I presented myself at the Council of Five Hundred, alone, unarmed, my head uncovered, just as the Elders had received and applauded me; I came to remind the majority of its wishes, and to assure it of its power.

The stilettos which menaced the deputies were instantly raised against their liberator; twenty assassins threw themselves upon me and aimed at my breast. The grenadiers of the Legislative Body whom I had left at the door of the hall ran forward, placed themselves between the assassins and myself. One of these brave grenadiers had his clothes pierced by a stiletto. They bore me out.

At the same moment cries of "Outlaw" were raised against the defender of the law. It was the fierce cry of assassins against the power destined to repress them.

They crowded around the president, uttering threats, arms in their hands; they commanded him to outlaw me; I was informed of this; I ordered him to be rescued from their fury, and six grenadiers of the Legislative Body secured him. Immediately afterwards some grenadiers of the Legislative Body charged into the hall and cleared it.

The factions, intimidated, dispersed and fled. The majority, freed from their attacks, returned freely and peaceably into the meeting hall, listened to the proposals on behalf of public safety, deliberated, and prepared the salutary resolution which is to become the new and provisional law of the Republic.

Frenchmen, you will doubtless recognize in this conduct the zeal of a soldier of liberty, a citizen devoted to the Republic. Conservative, tutelary, and liberal ideas have been restored to their rights through the dispersal of the rebels who oppressed the Councils.

John H. Stewart, ed., *A Documentary Survey of the French Revolution*. New York: Macmillan, 1951, pp. 763–65.

## Document 26: Napoléon Declares That the Revolution Is Over

*Having successfully completed his coup, Napoléon issued this short but profoundly significant proclamation on December 15, 1799. Note his frequent use of words like "rights," "equality," and "principles," long associated with the democratic ideals of the Revolution, but now intended to divert attention from the reality of his naked seizure of dictatorial power. In fact, the Revolution was only over in the official sense; its legacy would continue to transfigure France and the world for generations to come.*

Frenchmen!

A Constitution is presented to you.

It terminates the uncertainties which the provisional government introduced into external relations, into the internal and military situation of the Republic.

It places in the institutions which it establishes first magistrates whose devotion has appeared necessary for its success.

The Constitution is founded on the true principles of representative government, on the sacred rights of property, equality, and liberty.

The powers which it institutes will be strong and stable, as they must be in order to guarantee the rights of citizens and the interests of the State.

Citizens, the Revolution is established upon the principles which began it: It is ended.

Leon Bernard and Theodore B. Hodges, eds., *Readings in European History*. New York: Macmillan, 1958, pp. 349–50.

# Chronology

**1789**

May 5—The Estates General convenes at Versailles.

June 17—The third estate declares itself the National Assembly of France.

June 20—The members of the new Assembly swear to the so-called Tennis Court Oath.

June 27—The king requests that all three estates meet again and votes be counted individually rather than by group.

July 14—Paris's Bastille fortress surrenders to an angry mob.

Late July—The so-called Great Fear spreads through the countryside, igniting widespread peasant unrest and violence.

August 4—Responding to the peasant uprisings, the nobles in the Assembly give up most of their feudal rights.

August 27—The Assembly adopts the Declaration of the Rights of Man and Citizen.

October 2—Assembly leaders present the declaration to Louis for approval.

October 5–6—When Louis delays approval of the declaration, a crowd of Parisian women march to Versailles and demand that the royal family return with them to Paris.

**1791**

March 11—The pope condemns the French government's attack on the clergy.

June 20–24—Louis and his family attempt to escape France but are apprehended at Varennes.

October 1—The National Assembly having dissolved itself, the Legislative Assembly convenes its first session.

**1792**

April 20—France declares war on Austria.

August 10—Angry crowds break into the Tuileries Palace in Paris, forcing the royal family to flee to the safety of the Legislative Assembly.

September 20—A French army defeats the Prussians at Valmy.

September 21—The monarchy is abolished and the Legislative Assembly is replaced by the republican Convention.

December 15—The king is indicted on thirty-three counts of treason.

**1793**
January 21—The king is beheaded.

February 1—France declares war on Great Britain.

April—The Committee of Public Safety is formed and begins to assume its role as the chief organ of the Terror.

July—Robespierre joins the Committee of Public Safety.

July 13—Radical journalist Jean-Paul Marat is stabbed to death by a supporter of the Girondins.

September—The government passes the repressive Law of Suspects, facilitating the revolutionary tribunals of the Terror.

October 16—The former queen, Marie-Antoinette, is executed.

**1794**
April 6—The Jacobin leader Danton is executed.

July 26—Robespierre delivers his last speech to the Convention.

July 28—Robespierre is executed; the more moderate Thermidorian Reaction begins to gain control.

**1795**
August 22—The five-man ruling body known as the Directory is established.

**1796**
March—Napoléon Bonaparte becomes general of the French army in Italy.

**1797**
October 18—Napoléon concludes the Treaty of Campoformio with Austria.

**1798**

May 19—Napoléon begins his Egyptian expedition.

**1799**

August 22—Napoléon departs from Egypt.

October 16—Napoléon arrives in Paris.

November 10—Napoléon and his accomplices mount a coup of the government and he becomes First Consul.

December 15—Napoléon declares that the Revolution has come to an end.

# For Further Reading

## Collections of Original Documents Pertaining to the French Revolution

Frank M. Anderson, ed. and trans., *The Constitutions and Other Select Documents Illustrative of the History of France, 1789–1907.* Minneapolis: H.W. Wilson, 1908.

H. Beik, ed., *The French Revolution.* London: Macmillan, 1972.

Olivier Blanc, *Last Letters: Prisons and Prisoners of the French Revolution, 1793–1794.* Translated by Alan Sheridan. New York: Farrar, Straus & Giroux, 1987.

Edmund Burke, *Reflections on the Revolution in France.* Edited by Thomas H.D. Mahoney. Indianapolis: Bobbs-Merrill, 1955.

Alfred Cobban, ed., *The Debate on the French Revolution.* London: Adam and Charles Black, 1960.

E.L. Higgins, ed., *The French Revolution as Told by Contemporaries.* Boston: Houghton Mifflin, 1939.

Lynn Hunt, ed., *The French Revolution and Human Rights: A Brief Documentary History.* Boston: St. Martin's Press, 1996.

Darline G. Levy et al., eds., *Women in Revolutionary Paris, 1789–1795.* Urbana: University of Illinois Press, 1979.

John H. Stewart, ed., *A Documentary Survey of the French Revolution.* New York: Macmillan, 1951.

D.I. Wright, ed., *The French Revolution: Introductory Documents.* St. Lucia: University of Queensland Press, 1974.

## General Histories of the Revolution

Olivier Bernier, *Words of Fire, Deeds of Blood: The Mob, the Monarchy, and the French Revolution.* Boston: Little, Brown, 1989.

Crane Brinton, *A Decade of Revolution, 1789–1799.* New York: Harper and Row, 1934.

William Doyle, *Origins of the French Revolution.* Oxford: Oxford University Press, 1980.

———, *The Oxford History of the French Revolution.* Oxford: Clarendon Press, 1989.

Leo Gershoy, *The French Revolution and Napoléon.* New York: Appleton-Century-Crofts, 1964.

Norman Hampson, *The First European Revolution, 1776–1815.* New York: Harcourt, Brace, and World, 1969.

E.J. Hobsbawm, *The Age of Revolution.* New York: Praeger, 1969.

Peter Kropotkin, *The Great French Revolution, 1789–1793.* Translated by N.F. Dryhurst. New York: Schocken Books, 1971.

Claude Manceron, *Blood of the Bastille, 1787–1789.* Translated by Nancy Amphoux. New York: Simon and Schuster, 1989.

R.R. Palmer, *The World of the French Revolution.* New York: Harper and Row, 1971.

Gaetano Salvemini, *The French Revolution, 1788–1792.* Translated by I.M. Rawson. London: Jonathan Cape, 1954.

Simon Schama, *Citizens: A Chronicle of the French Revolution.* New York: Knopf, 1989.

D.M.G. Sutherland, *France, 1789–1815: Revolution and Counterrevolution.* New York: Oxford University Press, 1986.

## Social, Cultural, and Military Aspects of the Revolution

Jean-Paul Bertaud, *The Army of the French Revolution: From Citizen-Soldiers to Instrument of Power.* Translated by R.R. Palmer. Princeton, NJ: Princeton University Press, 1989.

Rafe Blaufarb, "The French Revolution: The Birth of European Popular Democracy?" *Comparative Studies in Social History,* vol. 37, July 1995, pp. 608–18.

Will and Ariel Durant, *Rousseau and Revolution.* New York: Simon and Schuster, 1967.

Norman Hampson, *A Social History of the French Revolution.* Toronto: University of Toronto Press, 1963.

Olwen H. Hufton, *Women and the Limits of Citizenship in the French Revolution.* Toronto: University of Toronto Press, 1992.

———, "Voilà la Citoyenne," *History Today,* vol. 39, May 1989, pp. 26–32.

Emmet Kennedy, *A Cultural History of the French Revolution.* New Haven, CT: Yale University Press, 1989.

Colin Lucas, "The Theory and Practice of Denunciation in the French Revolution," *Journal of Modern History,* vol. 68, December 1996, pp. 768–85.

John Markoff, "Violence, Emancipation, and Democracy: The

Countryside and the French Revolution," *American Historical Review*, vol. 100, April 1995, pp. 360–86.

John Paxton, *Companion to the French Revolution*. New York: Facts On File, 1988.

Michelle Perrot, ed., *From the Fires of Revolution to the Great War*. Vol. 4 of Philippe Ariès and Georges Duby, eds., *A History of Private Life*. Cambridge, MA: Harvard University Press, 1990.

J. Swann, "Cultural History of the French Revolution," *European History Quarterly*, vol. 23, October 1993, pp. 563–69.

Michel Vovelle, *The Fall of the French Monarchy, 1787–1792*. Translated by Susan Burke. Cambridge, England: Cambridge University Press, 1984.

Renée Waldinger et al., *The French Revolution and the Meaning of Citizenship*. Westport, CT: Greenwood Press, 1993.

**Personalities Who Shaped the Revolution**

N.N. Barker, "Let Them Eat Cake: The Mythical Marie Antoinette and the French Revolution," *Historian*, vol. 55, Summer 1993, pp. 709–24.

Henri Béraud, *Twelve Portraits of the French Revolution*. Translated by Madeleine Boyd. Boston: Little, Brown, 1928.

Bernard Faÿ, *Louis XVI, or The End of a World*. Translated by Patrick O'Brien. Chicago: Henry Regnery, 1968.

David P. Jordan, *The Revolutionary Career of Maximilien Robespierre*. New York: Macmillan, 1985.

Martin Lyons, *Napoléon Bonaparte and the Legacy of the French Revolution*. New York: St. Martin's Press, 1994.

R.R. Palmer, *Twelve Who Ruled: The Year of the Terror in the French Revolution*. New York: Atheneum, 1965.

J.M. Thompson, *Leaders of the French Revolution*. New York: Harper and Row, 1967.

**Impact and Legacy of the Revolution**

Peter Amann, ed., *The Eighteenth-Century Revolution: French or Western?* Boston: D.C. Heath, 1963.

Ferenc Fehér, ed., *The French Revolution and the Birth of Modernity*. Berkeley and Los Angeles: University of California Press, 1990.

R.K. Gooch, *Parliamentary Government in France: Revolutionary Origins, 1789–1791*. New York: Russell and Russell, 1960.

Lynn Hunt, "Forgetting and Remembering: The French Revolution Then and Now," *American Historical Review*, vol. 100, October 1995, pp. 1119–36.

Donald Kagan et al., *The Western Heritage, 1300–1815*. New York: Macmillan, 1983.

R.F. Leslie, *The Age of Transformation, 1789–1871*. New York: Harper and Row, 1967.

Norah Lofts and Margery Weiner, *Eternal France: A History of France from the French Revolution Through World War II*. Garden City, NY: Doubleday, 1968.

Arthur J. May, *A History of Civilization: The Mid–Seventeenth Century to Modern Times*. New York: Scribner, 1964.

R.R. Palmer, *The Age of Democratic Revolution: The Challenge*. Princeton, NJ: Princeton University Press, 1959.

George Rudé, *The French Revolution: Its Causes, Its History, and Its Legacy After 200 Years*. New York: Weidenfeld and Nicolson, 1988.

Jacques Solé, *Questions of the French Revolution: A Historical Overview*. Translated by Shelley Temchin. New York: Pantheon, 1989.

# Index